W9-CME-766

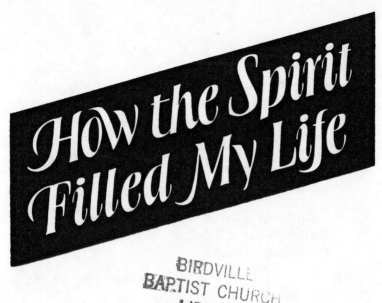

How the Spirit Filled My Life

Bertha Smith

BROADMAN PRESS
Nashville, Tennessee

To my dear friends in the Lord, Mrs. Hugh Armstrong and Mrs. Carlton Stokes of Memphis, who were so eager for me to write another book that they, in response to my call for prayer, left their husbands for three weeks to be companions to my sister Jennie, and to unitedly intercede for me while I went away from home to write.

To their husbands who graciously agreed, prayed, "batched" during the time, and provided their plane tickets,

I lovingly dedicate this volume.

4255–40
ISBN: 0–8054–5540–X

Library of Congress catalog card number: 73–87068
Dewey Decimal classification: B (Biography)
Printed in the United States of America

FOREWORD

Bertha Smith . . . Cowpens, South Carolina! Both name and place could easily been unfamiliar to most of us but for one thing—*the Holy Spirit filled her life.* God took a South Carolina girl and commissioned her as a missionary to the world. As Mordecai said to Esther, "Who knows whether you have not come to kingdom for such a time as this? Disillusionment and confusion are mounting in twentieth-century life. Bertha Smith's message is simple. Those who believe and apply it are discovering a simple life of victory.

Everywhere I go across the country I see people whose lives have been signally blessed through Bertha Smith's ministry. Their testimony is that no other human instrument has been used of God so much in their lives. This is my testimony!

Her life is proof of her message. God alone has been her strong tower through years in China, world travels, and continuous ministry past four score years. She is a spiritual fulfilment of the verses she claims as her promise from the Lord: "Those that be planted in the house of the Lord shall flourish in the courts of our God. They shall bring forth fruit in old age" (Ps. 92:13–14).

I have read the thrilling contents of these pages and can happily commend to you, the reader, the adventure of experiencing through them a season of refreshing from the hand of the Lord.

JACK R. TAYLOR

PREFACE

"GOD IS able to make all grace abound toward you; that ye, always having all sufficiency in all things, may abound to every good work" (2 Cor. 9:8).

With my speaking schedule, home responsibilities, and serving as Director, Secretary, and Treasurer of Peniel Prayer Center, which is being built by renovating a large residence across the street from my home, I felt that I could not undertake the writing of a book now.

Friends who have been filled, and my also knowing of the hunger which God has put into the hearts of his own on every hand, urged me to write. I thank Brother Jack Taylor who did not give up and helped me to choose from messages which he had heard, those which should be used in the book. He also had my first copy of the manuscript typed.

I have written with the prayer that all who read will no more hunger and thirst after righteousness, but will BE FILLED and overflowing.

BERTHA SMITH

CONTENTS

PART ONE

DIARY

"The light shall shine upon thy ways"
Job 22:28

"Our Lord calls to no special work:
He calls to himself."
O. Chambers

1

A FILLING OF NEW LIGHT

On a hot Sunday afternoon, June, 1907, when Mother and her eight sons and daughters sat on the front porch in our South Carolina home, my father came walking up the street carrying the suitcase of three guests. They were introduced to us as Rev. Troy and Luther Manness and Mr. McElrath, their singer.

Some days before, they had arrived in our town by train and put up at the hotel. When they asked the hotel manager to whom they should go to to get help in securing a place to put their tent for the gospel meetings, they were directed to my father. After enough conversation with them to see that they were trustworthy men, Father asked the mayor to let them use the vacant town lot in the center of town across the street from Father's store.

Meetings began Friday evening, to last through three Sundays. Everybody in town went, and we all wanted to go, but Father said, "Wait until you find out what those men are preaching!" Lo! We learned that he had been going to each service—Friday and Saturday evenings and Sunday afternoon. (There was no Sunday morning service.) He had, by that time, heard enough to be convinced that the men were there, as he expressed it, "for the good of the town."

Mother, with her four daughters, old enough to help and trained to do so, soon had a good supper for the thirteen who sat around our table with the cakes and pies which had been cooked on Saturday, as was our custom. Needless to say, we did not have to ask to go to the Sunday night service, nor any others.

By the time meetings had ended on the third Sunday evening the men had moved their tent to a Wesleyan churchyard eight miles out in the country. We were getting up and cooking a picnic basket of food for two meals to serve two buggies full of us who went daily to stay through three services. Crops were "laid by" and farmers had time to go to church all day.

Little did Father dream that his kindness to those strangers would mean that ten years later he would stand at the railway depot, fifty yards from the location of that tent, and say good-bye to one of his daughters leaving for China. When trying to ease his pain at the parting, I said, "Seven years will not be long and I will be back." He replied, "But I will not be here!"

When that first supper was over at our home, one of the preachers asked the four girls who stood together, "Are you all Christians?" "Yes," sister Jennie answered. I could never have answered in any other way after the time I had in becoming one; but what kind of Christians were we?

Home Church and Early Years

Growing up in a family where *yes* was *yes* and *no* was *no* with no arguing about it, and obedience and respect for our parents and older brothers and sisters was consistently instilled in us, I was a good girl. When children are taught properly at home, they show it in school. So, I never had a teacher whom I did not think was just wonderful, and I studied incessantly to please them. This meant that I was bragged on by the teachers, which I ate up! All who knew me referred to me as a "good girl," and I did not know any better than to believe it. I did everything possible to keep them approving of me.

The Baptist church, like most in small towns and the country in those days, had a pastor who served four churches. Our pastor lived forty miles away in the city of Greenville, and he came and went by train. When he came, it was his business to feed the saints. The deacons carried on the Wednesday evening prayer service (which was true to its name), the Sunday School, and later the Baptist Young People's Union.

When summer came, the church held a two-week revival, with two services daily. The twenty stores in town closed their doors for two hours for the forenoon service. If farmers came to town to shop, they could wait.

There were three classes of folk in the churches at that time: the warm-hearted Christians, the backsliders, and the class who were in those days called "the lost." Everybody went to church, the church being the social center, with nowhere else to go and nothing at home to keep one there.

The grand old man of God preacher, with tears rolling down his cheeks, pled with backsliders to confess their sins and come back into fellowship with Holy God. He pled with the lost to repent of their sins and flee from God's holy wrath to come, because it had been appointed unto man once to die, but after that the judgment! And while the man of God wept, preached the Word, and pled, saints prayed and the Holy Spirit moved.

Baptist churches did not have altar forms as the Methodist's did, but for two weeks in the year, we had plenty of repenting space. Those sitting on the front rows of benches across the church moved when the invitation was given, knowing that people would come. They stood in orderly lines down the aisles next to the walls and continued their share in singing to the unsaved, such as: "Come every soul by sin oppressed, there's mercy with the Lord." As more came, more benches were vacated, and sometimes half the church would be turned into a "mourner's bench!"

Mourn they did, as the Holy Spirit used the Word, to show them the exceeding sinfulness of sin, and they realized that only their life breath kept them out of an awful hell which had been made for the devil and his angels.

The backsliders were there too, like the prodigal of old, confessing to their Father their wandering away and doing as they pleased. They often wept sore as they realized what their sin had cost Holy God.

Struggles to Be Saved

I was ten years old when, one hot July night as I sat beside the second window from the front, the Word of the Lord went to my heart! For the first time I saw myself, at least a little glimpse of what I looked like, in the eyes of Holy God. While people called me a good girl, I would not do in his sight, who saw all the pride of my heart—the selfishness and the wanting to be first in everything, just to be praised by teachers. I wanted to make a hundred on all of my examinations, but I did not want anyone else to make a hundred! I had to excel! What an awful human being, a chip off the old block, Adam, after the devil entered into him!

Praise the Lord that we had a man of God for a pastor who knew that every human being was just like that, and he knew the remedy: Jesus Christ had come and died and taken in himself the sin of the human family; and that was what he proclaimed.

I wanted to go to the altar that first night, but on the evening before, a girl my age had gone and people said that she was too small, that she did not know what she was doing. Therefore, I did not dare go, but there was no peace of heart for me during the remainder of that meeting, or any other time.

The next year when the revival meeting began, I publicly announced myself a lost sinner by going to the altar and telling the Lord about my sins. In spite of the fact that I had been silently confessing for a year, that was my first chance to let other people know that I was conscious of my being one of the Lost.

No one was trained to do personal work at the altar. Only the pastor was at the altar to help people, and there were always so many older ones there, who took first place, that he never got to me.

I had to go on another year with my burden of sin, shedding many a tear in secret. Over and over again I told the Lord about my sins and pled for his cleansing.

About the third year, I was at the altar next to a woman whom the pastor came to help. It seemed to me that he talked with her a long time. He just stuck his head over toward me and said, "Just trust the Lord and he will save you." He was right, but I did not know what he meant by trusting the Lord. So that meeting came to an end with the cry of my heart being, "The summer is ended and I am not saved" (see Jer. 8:20).

When I went fifteen miles in the country to my grandmother's in the summer and attended their Big Meeting, I would just have to go to the altar. Occasionally we went to other nearby country churches for their summer meetings, and I could not but make my distress known. I went forward so much at my home church that I was afraid people would think that I was just going for the fun of it. I could have assured them that it certainly was not fun. Sometimes I would almost hold to the bench to keep from going forward but then I went home feeling worse then than when I went; and when I did go, it did no good! Oh, the wretched girl that I was!

Deceived . . . Still No Peace

After our pastor had been with us for fifteen years, he resigned and pastored another church in the community. When his revival meeting came, we went. I was among those at the altar wanting to be saved from hell. I was about fourteen by that time, and I suppose the pastor felt that I was old enough to have some attention. He said, "Bertha, if you will just trust the Lord, he will save you. Are you trusting him?"

I replied, "Yes, I am trusting the Lord."

He said, "Well, you are saved then."

(Now, what about one human being telling another that he is saved when the advisor cannot see whether or not a miracle has taken place inside?) He went back to the pulpit and asked anyone who had trusted the Lord at that service to stand. I stood, but I went home just as much in the dark as ever. I knew a good bit about the Lord, but he was away out yonder and I was here, under the burden of what I was in the sight of God, with no connection between us.

Born from Above

Two more summers passed, with a pastor who did no personal work. Then one last Sunday morning, after I had gone regularly to the altar as usual, the pastor asked if any at the front were ready to come to Jesus Christ and take him as Savior. For the first time, I saw that we come to the cross of Christ to be saved. Formerly I had not differentiated between God the Father and God the Son, and I did not know what was meant by "trusting God." Even though my advice had been right, all of the Godhead was God to me. I had been all those years trying to approach God the Father directly, no doubt even calling him "Father," when he is only the Father of those who believe his Son (Gal. 3:26). I learned that what the preachers meant by trusting God to save meant to trust God the Son, who settled my sin and my sinful self when he took my sins and me in his own body on the tree.

I was on the front seat, having gone forward at the first verse. I knew that I would go; there was no use to wait. It was but a step to where the pastor stood. I took it, gave him my hand to signify that I trusted in Christ's death to save me. By the time I took the second step, which was back to my seat, my years of burden of sin had rolled away, and the joy of the Lord filled my soul.

I think sometimes if the Lord could ever save anyone

the wrong way, he would have saved me! He must really have been sorry for me. I praise him that he never let go, but made that conviction stronger and stronger until someone said enough about Christ's death, or Christ being the Savior, for me to lay hold on what he had done for me. There is no direct road from the sinful heart to God the Father. I tried to make one, but it did not work! My sin was settled at the cross, and through Christ's death I at last came, which is the only way that anyone gets to him.

I went home so thrilled, and so sorry for everyone else who was not in tune with the Lord, that I did not want any of that good Sunday dinner. My parents and two older sisters and both older brothers were church members and one brother and sister younger were old enough to be saved, so I just had to go to my place of prayer by the trunk in the walk-in closet in my room and plead with God for the family and for friends and neighbors.

But that joy wore off. Before many months I showed no more of the fruit of the Spirit in my life than the rest of my family, for whom I prayed that glorious Sunday when I passed out of death into life. I well knew to whom I belonged, even though at times I knew that I was not pleasing him. When the visiting preacher, Brother Manness, asked, "Are you girls all Christians?" I knew that Sister Jennie answered right, but I longed for something more of the Lord whom I knew!

When the Spirit Visited My Family

We found that the well-bred Manness brothers were sons of a Methodist preacher in Greensboro, North Carolina, who had education, books, and twelve children. Even though they are "cheaper by the dozen," the two brothers could not afford to go to college. Therefore they attended Dr. Knapp's Bible School in Cincinnati, where they received good training. At breakfast, when we tried to decide which one of them was the better preacher, we usually agreed on the last one we heard.

They preached that people who are saved belong to the Lord—mind, body, and soul—that we should acknowledge that fact, confess all of our sins of failing the Lord, so as to be cleansed, and then hand over ourselves and let the Holy Spirit fill us. We would then be empowered to live to please the Lord all the time. We had never heard anything like that.

First, my second sister had her life made over by taking our copy of their new hymn book to the central office where she was working that summer. While reading the hymns, the Holy Spirit so revealed the truth of one to her heart that she came home with a testimony of having gone all the way with the Lord.

That so moved Mother that she was soon one of those at the altar seeking all that the Lord had for her. Up to that time we had family prayer only when the pastor spent the night with us and led it. When Mother was down at that altar before the Lord seeking the fullness of his Spirit, the Lord asked something of her, which was that she start family prayer. For a quiet woman of the home who had never even given a testimony in public or prayed aloud, that was a demand! She struggled that hot day until she had completely ruined her lovely lavender silk blouse. The change in her, how marvelous! Soon it was sister Jennie at the altar, and brother Lester, a third-year college student

who discovered that he had been baptized at twelve
years of age because he was convicted of sin but never
had been saved. Down on his knees there, he cried to
the Lord, a lost sinner, and when the Lord met him, he
declared that he joined a Baptist church at the age of
twelve because he was convicted of sin and wanted to
be a better boy.

Bertha's turn came too, and time after time I went
down wanting to be a better Christian.

Hungry for More

A message on Romans 12:1-2 was used of the Lord to
make clear to me just what the dear Lord expected: "I
beseech you therefore brethren [saved people], by the
mercies of God, that ye present your bodies a living
sacrifice, holy, acceptable unto God, which is your reasonable service. And be not conformed to this world:
but be ye transformed by the renewing of your mind,
that ye may prove what is that good, and acceptable,
and perfect will of God."

I did not know then as much as I learned later about
offerings presented to God, especially in the consecra-
tion of the sons of Aaron to become priests (Lev. 8).
First, they had to be born of the priesthood; next, they
had to be bathed, typical of cleansing; then clothed in
pure white linen, which must have represented the
righteous standard which Holy God requires.

In those days Baptist churches did not have rededica-
tion meetings every few months, or call for people
every Sunday to come down and rededicate. I did not
have that kind of church background. However, I had
learned from that sermon on dedication (Rom. 12:1-2)
and from the Word that the sacrifice for dedication had

to be without blemish—a perfect specimen of sheep—
before it could be acceptable. I had for days been confessing all the sins that I knew about, and seeing that
the altar meant handing self over to live for the Lord. I
knew just what to do.

When the invitation was given, I went immediately,
and there I had a business transaction with my Lord. I
handed myself over to him for anything that he might
choose for me. His Word was that this was not something special, but only what was expected of me because the Lord saved me. It was "my reasonable service," not too much to ask.

I was ready to quit being conformed to the world,
but by a changed mind toward the world (my environ-
ment) I would prove the will of the Lord for my life,
which would be good, acceptable to me, and perfect. It
did not take long for me to do this, so prepared was my
heart. I handed myself over, accepting from the Lord
whatever he might bring or not bring into my life. I
literally put myself on the altar to live for the Lord
only.

Filled with the Holy Spirit

The congregation still sang invitation hymns, but
there was no use for me to kneel there longer. I had
done what the Word told me to do, and I knew that
the One who died for me could be trusted to do all
that had been promised. I got up and returned to my
seat. By the time I got there, joy unspeakable was filling my soul! I knew that the Holy Spirit, who had come
into my heart when I was saved and had wanted to fill
me those two years but could not unless I knew how to
let him, had taken over.

I thought that the sin principle in me had been removed, eradicated, and I would never sin any more. The Holy Spirit so magnified Christ that I did not sin for a good while! Or rather I was not convicted of sins by the Holy Spirit. Certainly he saw much in me that grieved him, but he would rule those out as he saw me able to take it.

Results of Being Filled

"I am full of power by the spirit of the Lord" (Mic. 3:8).

When the Holy Spirit began to magnify Christ, all worldly pleasure lost its flavor. No longer did I want to talk like the world or look like worldly people. I took off my jewelry, my pretty clothes with the laces, ribbons, and feathered and flowered hats, and I wore the very plainest clothes. In nothing did I want to attract attention to myself. (While I am sure that the Lord was leading, I doubt now that he led me to go as far as I did go.) That was the way the Wesleyans dressed, and they were the only Spirit-filled people whom I knew for a pattern. (I learned later that modest pretty clothes not only keep me from ever thinking of how I am dressed, but has the same effect in other people who have to look at me.)

The Bible Became a New Book

I signed up for a correspondence course with Dr. Knapp's Bible School and was enjoying what I could understand until sister Jennie looked at some of the lessons and said, "This is too deep for you! It is a preacher's course."

Passages came alive that I had committed to memory

when a child. I added many verses, paragraphs, and chapters to these. At school the principal came up to an unused classroom one day at recess time and found me sitting on an almost cold radiator on the floor reading my New Testament. He just turned on more heat and went out.

I Wanted Everybody to Be Saved

The Lord laid on my heart twenty unsaved young people about my age. I began to pray for them by name daily and saw eighteen of them saved that same summer. The nineteenth was saved some years later. The other one moved away and I lost contact.

Prayer Became Communion with God

Prayer became communion with God not only in private but with others of like mind. I was only in the ninth grade, because formerly our school had gone through only eight grades. I was described by the others in school as "Bertha has religion." The church seemed cold to me, but my joy was in attending a woman's prayer meeting on Wednesday afternoon where a "Spirit-filled" woman gave the meat of the Word, after which we joined our hearts in praise and intercession.

2

FAILURE, THEN FULLNESS

As time went on I began to discover that the sin principle in me was not removed. It too often exerted itself and I did not know what to do about it. Needless to say, I was grieved over every accidental sin which was a grief to the Holy Spirit within me. I constantly prayed to get back the glorious experience of the first filling. Sometimes the Lord in his marvelous mercy did restore perfect peace and a measure of joy, but it was not sustained and, needless to say, there was no power for service.

While I continually tried to lead someone to the Savior I did not see many brought in genuine conviction to the foot of the cross become willing for Jesus Christ to reign over them. Being busy in church work did not completely satisfy.

During four years in college, though active in all forms of Christian organizations on campus, I led only one classmate to the Lord.

While teaching in public school, my heart broke over lost pupils, but I did not have power to win them, even though I most faithfully kept my quiet time with the Lord and his Word.

Sometimes after much confession of failure and prayer I received another uplift, but what to do with the old self I did not know.

I Went to China

I studied for two years at Southern Baptist Theological Seminary, under the old men of God there who were marvelous teachers of the Word. Then I went to China, but I had not discovered how to live victoriously all the time over the old self. I was wholly the Lord's and living there only that people might know my Savior, but how the Lord could get through me to numbers of them I did not know. Not knowing continuous filling, I was unable to lead other missionaries into what I had experienced. They only described me as having "good religion." The crowds of lost people would have broken my heart and no doubt my health had the Lord not come to my rescue.

A saint of the Lord in California, Mr. Milton Stewart, knowing the heart hunger of missionaries, left a sum of money in his will with which to build four summer conference centers in four sections of China, where missionaries could go for one dollar per day for ten days for spiritual refreshing. Most of the speakers were from America, being assisted by suitable missionaries on the field like Miss Ruth Paxson and Miss Marie Monsen.

One way in which I cooperated with our Foreign Mission Board was in the custom of vacation! Every summer I went away for a few weeks and always went to a conference. During my second summer in China, the speaker for the North China Conference was Dr. R. A. Torrey. He spoke twice daily on the Spirit-filled life. What an uplift to come back to the filling of former years! However, my old self still occasionally bobbed up.

The third summer, Dr. Charles G. Trumbull, editor of the *Sunday School Times* and Miss Ruth Paxson were the speakers. What a team they were! Miss Paxson was an expert in showing from the Word of God the old nature: its loves, its pride, its desires for self-expression, and its ability to dedicate itself to Jehovah God and work hard thinking it was serving the Lord.

Dr. Trumbull's message was "Christ in You, the Hope of Glory." Christ had been in me since I had been saved, but I did not know that. All that I knew was that he was along by my side. The truth that Christ was living inside of us had much more meaning than just being beside us. In fact, we were so thrilled in the thought that Christ was living inside of us that the old self did not bother us so much. Christ in us was stronger than our sinful natures, stronger than the other person's human nature and stronger than the devil himself. Therefore, life was never the same!

Needless to say, the new blessing created in our hearts a deep desire for the Chinese Christians to know that Christ was living in them.

We missionaries prayed together at every opportunity! There came a hunger—in fact, a definite burden —to pray for reviving in the churches, in our private devotions, missionary prayer meetings, and the church meetings. After a few years, the burden became so great that in consultation with the Chinese pastor in the city where I worked, a day of prayer for reviving was set aside the first day of every month. All who could do so went to the church house at nine o'clock each of those mornings and prayed until twelve, then returned back at two in the afternoon until five. They had no speaking. A different leader each hour chose a hymn, read a Bible passage, and directed the praying.

Knowing that we prayed within the will of God, we expected a true new work of God in the hearts of leaders and lay members. "If my people, which are called by my name, shall humble themselves, and pray, . . . I will hear from heaven" (2 Chron. 7:14).

While the national government of China was being established, and as various provincial leaders strived for leadership and fought with one another, the city of Nanking was burned by the victorious army from the South.

The next day all missionaries received a telegram from American consulates with the message, "Proceed to the coast at once!" Our North China group suddenly was called away from the work we loved more than we loved our own lives. We packed up in the port cities of Chefoo and Tsingtao. We were grieved over the break with our work, never dreaming what blessings the Lord had in store for us.

Being unable to work with the Chinese in Chefoo where we were not known, because of the strong communist influence, we had plenty of time to pray together. We started out from eight till nine each day, but soon were praying until eleven, or even until twelve o'clock. At first our prayers were centered on the Chinese Christians and their danger of being persecuted by the communists. Soon we were praying for ourselves and asking the Lord not to let us miss what he had to teach us in permitting that interruption in our work.

After a few weeks, he began to show us our consecrated selves with all of our faithful dedication and hard work for him.

One of our number, Miss Jane Lide, had just returned from a winter spent in Southern California where she attended a Bible Class for several months, where only one subject was taught: "Christ Our Life."

This was something more than just having Christ inside of us, this was Christ enthroned! Christ reigning!

New teaching came to us along with the "Christ Reigning," which was that the old self should be assigned to the position of death.

In learning how we could keep Christ enthroned, we majored for days on Romans 6. Dual governments do not work with the Lord. One personality must be in control. We saw, as we studied and trusted the Holy Spirit to reveal truth, that we had been in God's sight in the position of death since we were saved.

Holy God cannot fellowship with anything that comes from the devil, until it is punished. That punishment is death; therefore, he had to put us to death (of course, not actually dead, but assigned to the position of death in his sight) before he in all of his holiness could come into our hearts.

Therefore he arranged for Christ to die in our stead. We did not know that, and for years we had been trying to crucify ourselves.

The gracious Lord knew that we met the first day of every month and prayed for six hours: "Lord, revive the church members of North China." He listened and answered in the only way that he could. Missionaries had to see themselves as dedicated selves working hard for the Lord because they loved him. Seeing our failure made us heartsick. We not only were shown our failure in work, but our lack of being holy. There was no conviction for lack of work. We had evermore put in time, some of us fifteen hours a day. But the Holy Spirit revealed sin even in our work, showing pride in the number of the ones we led to make "decisions" and prepared for baptism.

We had to admit that we often only had deceived people and caused the pastor to be guilty of the sin of burying people alive, since they had never entered into Christ's death and had his death charged to them.

As we missionaries searched our hearts in the light of Christ living his life in us, instead of ourselves living it, we realized that we could never do anything for the Lord. The only way that we could be acceptable to him would be for Christ to express himself through us (Col. 3:1-4).

Certainly our methods of work were transformed when we realized that no one ever is saved except by a miracle of the Holy Spirit. The Holy Spirit works miracles by using the written Word. We *saw* that people would not be saved by our influencing their wills to decide for Christ. The Holy Spirit would use the Word when presented to the mind to show the sinfulness of man's human nature in contrast to Jehovah God's holy standard for him, and show that man deserves death— eternal separation from God.

We *learned* to wait until the Holy Spirit dangles people over hell and moves them to call upon God in repentance. When they took refuge in Christ's death, they could receive the gift of faith from God to receive the living Lord into their hearts.

Therefore, we realized that our work for the Lord

was being tuned by prayer, so that we would be brought in contact with people who would repent if they had opportunity. We were then to give the Word of God, trusting the Holy Spirit to reveal it to the heart. What different tools we became!

We were now in a position to prove our deaths to ourselves. This gave the ability to accept pruning. The Lord kept cutting here and there to get us in shape.

During the remaining weeks in Chefoo, the Lord let us know that he had taken over, so to speak, and would show us up to ourselves in order that we might gladly say yes to all the changes he might want to make in us.

I was years learning that I cannot crucify myself. God put me in the position of death by charging the death of his Son to me when I took refuge in his death, or entered into his death to be saved.

For that reason I was buried in a grave of water to announce publicly what I had done in my heart. Instead of now praying, "Lord, crucify Me," I thank him that he not only took my sins in his own body on the tree, but took me there when he went in my stead.

I struggled over Galatians 2:20: "I am crucified with Christ; nevertheless I live, yet not I, but Christ liveth in me," and the truth of Romans 6. If Paul could be dead, why could not I? Why did the old self arise at the most unexpected times and cause me trouble?

Christ Our Life

One day I said, "Lord, since you count me dead in your Son, I will count myself dead in him, no matter how much alive I may be appearing!"

When I began to praise the Lord for having taken me to death, I was "faithing" myself dead. This gave the Holy Spirit a chance to so control the old self that it was ineffective over me. No more "death struggles."

It is the business of the Holy Spirit to take care of the old self and to magnify Christ through our personalities. When he is ungrieved in us and can fill up all the space that is left when the "Big I" moves out, he is free to do his work. Life then becomes glorious!

We can then use the term "filled with the Holy Spirit" to mean that there is only one personalty there, who is the third person of the Trinity.

From Chefoo, missionaries returned to their various centers of work with a new message: "Them that call on the Lord out of a pure heart" (2 Tim. 2:22).

The tragedy of sin in the life of a saved person became our major subject.

Pastors were the first, then lay workers, followed by other church leaders to be led the same way of the missionaries in brokenness, followed by confession, restitution, choosing to live dead to self with Christ enthroned and the Holy Spirit filling.

What joy our church services became with whole congregations of saved people on praying ground! What miracles the Holy Spirit wrought in the saved and unsaved!

Needless to say, "rivers of living water" began to flow from all who kept cleansed.

Within a few short years the membership of the churches multiplied ten times and most of the churches had a waiting list of young people waiting their turn to get into the seminary to be trained for full-time Christian work. What joy to be a representative of the Lord among them!

The revival continued for ten years, until the Japanese army invaded North China.

Dr. Cal Guy, head of the missions department of Southwestern Baptist Seminary, Fort Worth, Texas, calls that the greatest revival in modern church history. (See *The Shantung Revival* by Dr. Charles L. Culpepper, Sr., and *Go Home and Tell* by Bertha Smith.)

One result of our personal reviving was that we all became singers. We sang individually and delighted to do so in groups, praising The Lord for all he had done for us and was doing in us at the time.

Our favorite hymn was Dr. A. B. Simpson's "Himself" (summer of 1927). We sang this song daily, as nothing else could so clearly express our new life.

Once it was the blessing, now it is the Lord;
Once it was the feeling, now it is His Word;
Once His gift I wanted, now, the Giver own;
Once I sought for healing, now Himself alone.

Once 'twas painful trying, now 'tis perfect trust;
Once a half salvation, now the uttermost;
Once 'twas ceaseless holding, now he holds me fast;
Once 'twas constant drifting, now my anchor's cast.

Once 'twas busy planning, but now 'tis trustful prayer
Once 'twas anxious caring, now He has the care;
Once 'twas what I wanted, now what Jesus says;
Once 'twas constant asking, now 'tis ceaseless praise.

Once it was my working, His it hence shall be;
Once I tried to use Him, now He uses me;
Once the power I wanted, now the Mighty One;
Once for self I labored, now for Him alone.

Refrain:

All in all forever, Jesus will I sing;
Everything in Jesus, and Jesus everything.

PART TWO

A NEW ASSIGNMENT

3

CHANGE OF FIELDS

"Mine age is as nothing before thee" (Psalm 39:5).

An Old Woman

Only the Lord can know how it hurt to reach the age of seventy and have to give up the work to which he had called me in China. He comforted me in the wee small hours one morning by letting me know that he wanted me to come home and help bring a reviving to Southern Baptist churches, in order that the whole world might know of the Savior.

For the first few years after retirement I served on programs, which is a good work, and spoke somewhere every Sunday—at most, twice to the same group. After a few years of this, I became convinced that revival in people's hearts would not come without having more consecutive teaching on their own sin and failure to live up to God's standard for his own.

In 1962, the Woman's Missionary Union of the Southern Baptist Convention held its first prayer retreat, preceding their annual meeting in San Francisco, for two whole days. They planned to celebrate their seventy-fifth anniversary the following year and wanted a program which would glorify the Lord and advance interest in missions. Dr. Davis led the Bible devotions for the retreat while I brought messages on prayer.

From that time on the WMU advocated prayer retreats. I led many of them.

Christian Life Conferences

"He wakeneth mine ear to hear as the learned" (Isa. 50:4).

Churches then began to invite me to speak for a week at a time. For a name, I called my week-long meetings "Christian Life Conferences." The week begins on Sunday morning and goes through Friday evening, with three services on Sunday (one of which was Training Union hour), and two daily services each week day.

When the Southern Baptist Convention prepared for the Crusade of the Americas, those setting up the crusades started inviting me to lead associations of pastors in prayer retreats several weeks in advance, in preparation for their parts in the Crusade.

The Lord gave me a message relative to each group. "Cause My People to Know Their Sins," from Isaiah 58:1.

The first few messages to each group for the last ten years has been the same—that of giving the Word of God, for the Holy Spirit to show the hearers their sins and how they are failing God.

My purpose in going is to help get the hearers filled with the Holy Spirit as equipment for their service. I have learned that the first step is to lead the hearers to get clean enough for the Holy Spirit to fill.

"If a man shall steal an ox . . . he shall restore five oxen for an ox" (Ex. 22:1).

Restitution

A few years ago I went to Temple Church in Fay-
etteville, North Carolina to lead a Christian Life Conference.

On Sunday morning between Sunday School and
church, a fine looking man about thirty came and said,
"Miss Bertha, I am absolutely brokenhearted! I had
looked forward to your coming for a year. I am guilty
of committing the same sins over and over and have to
get on my knees every night and confess these sins to
God, until I am embarrased to mention them to him
again!

"I have read your book, *Go Home and Tell*," he
continued, "and I thought that when you came you
would be able to show me how to live victoriously over
these besetting sins. Therefore, I had planned my vacation for this week so that I could be at home to attend
the meetings. Now, last night a telegram came saying to
report for duty Monday morning." Of course, the devil
intended to keep the man from becoming useful to
God.

At that church I did something which I do not ordi-
narily do. The pastor assured me before the Tuesday
morning service that some would be present who
wanted prayer help and were ready for it. It usually
takes until about Thursday morning to get a group
ready for prayer. Twenty women filed by the pulpit
and back to the prayer room. When I went back, they
first began to share with me what they wanted the Lord
to do for them.

One charming young woman, a pastor's wife said,
"Miss Bertha, I am perfectly awful! I will be reading
and come across a nice-sounding phrase and underscore

it, saying to myself, 'This will sound nice in my next public prayer.' Oh, Miss Bertha, I am just awful." Of course, the dear Lord knew that she was telling the truth, for he was showing her the awfulness of her proud heart. She humbled herself before him and was cleansed and delivered from sin-cancer in her heart. What a humble, joyous Christian she is today!

The wife of the pastor of the local church was also among the twenty who thought herself "awful!" Her trouble was carrying the big load of the church. With the husband she had, she needed only to sit and praise the Lord every sentence of his messages, but instead she bore on her soulders the responsibility of every sermon and, in fact, all that he did. Continously in her mind was the question, "Will the people approve of that?"

She laid the burden of that church and her husband over on the Lord, and left it there. She was so enlightened by the Holy Spirit that she saw her sin in taking upon herself the responsibility of her husband and the church. With two small children and the other burdens, she was just about ready to have a nervous breakdown.

She had heard the Lord say, "Come unto me, all ye that labour and are heavy laden, and I will give you rest." With this promise of rest for her soul, when she had gotten her sins all transferred to the cross of Christ and then her old self assigned to the place of death, she just turned all of the burdens over to the Lord.

She went home so lighthearted and absolutely detached that in a few days' time the pastor told me that he had a new wife. He said, "I really believe that she would have had a breakdown within a few weeks had you not come." He could not praise the Lord enough for what he was doing for her, and for others in the church.

On Sunday morning I had asked him to let the invitation be to the whole congregation, which would be going home and meeting with the Lord alone after lunch to list their sins against him. The pastor had said to himself, "This is a splendid plan for my people; they need to face up to their sins!" By Thursday, so many had gone all the way with the Lord that the pastor was delighted. Somehow he had not taken in the fact that at his church I could only stay through Thursday evening, and he had announced meetings through Friday. Since people were coming from other churches, we could not close Thursday, so he had to prepare messages for Friday morning and evening.

By Thursday evening when he took me home, he was about to the end of himself. Sure enough, he said, "I have to list my own sins today; I have never before known that I am such a sinner. My heart is so hungry for the fullness of the Holy Spirit, I can hardly stand it! Why didn't I see myself earlier in the week? I cannot be filled with the Holy Spirit for two more weeks, and I do not see how I can stand to wait!"

He had sinned when a teen-age boy in his hometown, but had not taken the blame as the guilty party. All those years he had let the other boy bear the blame for what he himself had done. He said, "I must return to my hometown and straighten out those things, and I cannot go for two weeks." When I asked if he could phone his confession, he replied that too many people were involved, that he would have to go himself. Needless to say, I went into the house sorely grieved for him.

My hostess was a woman whom I had seen for years

at Ben Lippen Victorious Life Conferences and other deeper life conferences. In fact, she was always there. When I first reached her home as a guest, I asked why she attended all the Bible conferences, was it because she was filled with the Holy Spirit or because she wanted to be? She replied, "Because I want to be filled. My heart is so hungry for all that the Lord has for me that I can hardly endure it."

It did not take long for her to be filled. I am sorry to say the husband was a satisfied deacon of many years, an upright, honest man with never an interest in anything more than he had experienced when he was converted as a boy.

After the hostess was filled, I had her as a prayer partner at home before and after services. When I went in that Thursday night, there was no sleep for a while; I was asking and believing that the Lord would not keep that young pastor waiting two whole weeks before filling him. He knew that he was going to go back and make that wrong right. So my hostess and I united our hearts and called upon the Lord to fill him, even that night.

He went home to his study to prepare a message for Friday morning, but just couldn't. He began crying to the Lord to be filled before he had to go into the pulpit again! The Lord in his faithfulness met him. The next morning when he came at six A.M. to take me to the airport, he was on cloud nine! Literally bubbling over. The congregation did not need a message Friday morning or evening. They were so full of joy, that all they needed was a chance to express it by word, song, and prayer. That young man is in another state now, feeding the flock and leading them on with the Lord.

Strength to Die

"Though your sins be as scarlet, they shall be as white as snow" (Isa. 1:18).

A few years ago when at Security, Colorado, near a big military training camp, some of the young men being trained to go to Vietnam came to the meetings. One dear handsome one from North Carolina, expecting to preach, had left college when half through to get his military training over. At the time he served as assistant to a chaplain. However, he confessed his service as useless. Not being victorious over sin in his own life, how could he help other men out of bondage? Young men, some of whom were appointed soon to die, needed help which he could not give.

He humbled himself at the foot of the cross, transferred his sins to the Lord, and gave up his sinful self. He then so exalted Christ that the Holy Spirit filled him. In prayer, afterwards, he said, "Lord, I thank you for giving me strength to die!" Again when praying he said, "Lord, I do praise you for teaching me how to live dead!"

From that same group came one who wanted help privately. No wonder! He had to confess bondage to the sin for which the city of Sodom was destroyed. He saw that if God was the civil ruler of this nation today that he would be put to death for that sin.

We two were kneelng at the front seat in the church, empty except for the pastor who was in the back praying. When he had brought out that awful blackness from the pit of hell against his body, against the bodies of other men, and above all against Holy God, and before the angels, my instantaneous response was, "In the name and upon the authority of the resurrected all-powerful Jesus Christ, I command you, homosexual demon, come out of his man!"

The young man hollered out and fell backwards. He then resumed his kneeling position and poured out his sins in confession at the foot of the cross, where they were washed white.

Condemnation

For another Christian Life Conference, I was assigned to stay in the home of a young deacon whose wife was a jewel. The pastor and wife had met me at the airport on Saturday afternoon. He said that since they were building a new auditorium and the noise of the workmen during the day would disturb, he did not announce day meetings. He knew that all who could attend would be present Sunday and could hear any announcement made, so he waited for my arrival to decide what to do.

When the pastor and wife were ready to leave the deacon's home, I asked if they had time to pray with me for the Sunday meetings. My hostess suggested that we go to my bedroom since the three daughters might be coming home soon.

We knelt around that Hollywood bed to pray. When each of them had poured out his heart for the Sunday meeting, I joined them and knew, "This is it! Our day services will be praying meetings here."

I suggested that no announcement be made, that they just quietly tell individuals whom they knew were on praying ground to come. The next morning we had eight.

One man who worked at night gave up half his sleeping time to come to pray daily. And well did he

need it! He confessed his failure to live in victory, and
with weeping begged us to pray that he would be given
strength to stand his wife's poor housekeeping. That
man got into praying tune the first morning.

The next morning a hungry-hearted woman or two
did the same. On through the week, one or two a day
went all out for the Lord. Two precious young matrons
invited me to eat lunch with them that we might have
a quiet time together. One had no assurance of salvation, even though active in the church. In fact, she was
sure by the time we finished lunch that she had never
met the Lord at the cross. She went down before him
and evermore humbled herself and entered into his
death. Of course, that was preparation for leading her
to assign the "Old Man" to death and so enthrone
Christ so that she could appropriate the Holy Spirit to
fill her. What a joy they became the remainder of the
week!

I believe it was Monday when my hostess was filled,
and in a day or two, her husband—who could not attend day prayer meetings—was helped by the wife to
be filled.

How happy he was for a few days, just working in
the blessed light of the Lord's presence! Lo, about Friday, he had an "accident"! His work was selling and installing electric household equipment. He and one of
his clerks were in a home installing a washing machine.
It was white, an opening at the top, with a black agitator. He forgot that he no longer was to try to attract attention to himself and, wanting to make his attendant
laugh, he said, "You know this washing machine just
describes our situation in the South! A white environ-
ment with a black agitator!" The other man laughed,

but in a moment the speaker was smitten in his heart. What could he do? He knew that he had grieved the Holy Spirit. He just couldn't stand it! In another person's home he could not go to a closet to confess that sin and lay it on Christ, and claim his forgiveness, cleansing, and restoration, but he had to do something! He could not endure that misery until he could go home to his place of prayer that night. He rushed out to his station wagon, opened the hood and stuck his head under it, and was in the closet! There he cried to his Lord, pouring out his remorse and brokenheartedness. He placed that sin on the Lord, again assigned the old self to his place of death, and once more put the Lord on the throne of his heart and life. He asked the grieved Holy Spirit to refill him, to keep him in the place of death, and to magnify Jesus Christ through his personality. Needless to say, he learned from this experience to trust the Lord to keep him from accidental sins.

The GA Leader That Could Not Pray

On Sunday night at church, one of the first to be invited to attend the morning prayer meetings was the GA leader. She frankly declined, saying, "I will not be there! You people all pray aloud at your prayer meetings, and I cannot pray before people. I was not brought up to pray aloud. Growing up in a Baptist church in the North, I was not even saved until some Southern Baptist church members who had a testimony went up there and joined my church. Seeing that they had a personal acquaintance with the Lord and I did not, I went to them for help and was saved. But not having the background of you Southern people, I just cannot pray in the presence of others; therefore, I will not be at the prayer meetings."

I had breakfast with my hostess each morning, and went to homes for lunch. I fasted at the dinner hour in accordance with my custom when leading meetings.

On Thursday it was the turn of the GA leader to have me at her home for lunch. At the table I asked her if she had made her sin list. She said, "Yes, I had twelve sins!" I thought that she had gotten off lightly! I next asked if any of those twelve sins were against anyone else and required apology. "No!" she said. "I have not sinned against anyone else, only against the Lord."

My next question was, "Do you have children?" She replied, "A son eight years old who is at school." I asked, "Have you ever punished him when you were angry?" Her countenance fell as she meekly replied, "I am sure that I have." I further asked, "Do you not think that you are due him an apology for using your authority over him and punishing him when you are not calm enough to first pray and lead him to see his sin?"

That afternoon, after having made apologies to her son, she remembered that she once had some words with a woman in the church. She called her and begged her forgiveness. The next morning she had to call my hostess and apologize to her for something that had come between them in the past. She then added, "I will be at your prayer meeting this morning!" She was there and volunteered to lead in prayer three times!

Deliverance From Smoking

In one church I visited, I spoke at Training Union, since students have to study weekday evenings. Instead of an invitation at the close of the service, I suggested that all go home and list on a paper all their known sins. Monday morning, at the end of the first day, many were under conviction of sin. A young man temporarily assisting the pastor while waiting to enter seminary the next year to prepare for the ministry went to the pastor on Monday morning and told him that he had never been born of the Spirit. The pastor sat down and shared passages of Scripture on what Christ had done for him. Seeing that they meant nothing to the young man, he then took him at his word and turned to passages on the exceeding sinfulness of the human heart and God's holiness. When the young man was so crushed over his sins that he could not stand it any longer, the pastor showed him that God the Father would count his sins on his Son when he himself put them there.

When the young man had poured out all known sin in sincere confession and thanked the Lord that he had taken the punishment for all that he deserved, and because of his shed blood he could be right with God, he received the living Lord into his heart.

He jumped up and rushed out to other members of the staff to testify and praise the Lord. When the church hostess heard the testimony, she was smitten with conviction and went to the pastor for help. Before the afternoon was over she, too, was going to one staff member after the other telling them how wonderful it was to be saved. At the Monday evening service, both gave testimonies that brought heart-searching to others.

By the morning prayer time on Tuesday, other staff members, Sunday School and WMU workers—while knowing that they were saved—were getting miserable over the way they were not living out the gospel.

These were still adding to their sin lists daily, as more conviction came, and day by day others were joined to the miserable group. A number were so convicted of smoking that they started pleading with the Lord for deliverance.

As some prayed through to death to self and the enthroning of Christ, and let the Holy Spirit fill them, they wanted to tell others. We began to have one minute long testimonies, a few at each service, so that others would know to whom to go for help.

I had sorely grieved to see on the week's calendar a Halloween party for Friday evening. What kind of a church or young people's director could make such plans when Friday would be the closing service for meetings which had been planned for nearly a year? All that I could do was to speak to a few who had been filled and get them to praying with me about it.

About Tuesday, the pastor's youngest of four daughters began to get miserable over her own state before the Lord. I did not major on salvation, just talked about how sin separates us from Holy God and so grieves the Holy Spirit that he is not free to help us.

The dear girl went to her mother with the question as to whether or not she was saved. Her mother advised her to recall her salvation experience at baptism. But that had taken place when she was too young to recall anything that would help.

When the father came home and found his daughter in distress, he knew exactly what to do. They sat down with the Word of God and from it he showed her that we are by nature sinners, what Jesus did about those sins, and how God the Father laid them all on his Son

(Isa. 53). Then he showed what we have to do for his death to be charged to us. She was so sure that God was away yonder and she here in her sins with no connections between them that she went down on her knees in confession at the cross and met the Lord for the first time.

During the next morning service the pastor, music director, and educational director poured out their hearts in undescribable weeping and confession, followed by a number of others. I believe that was the day that we stayed on our knees there until one in the afternoon.

Before the day was over, daughter number three was miserable from conviction, describing herself as a good-for-nothing, full-of-sin Christian.

The father led her to transfer all of her sins and her sinful self to the cross of Christ and to enthrone the living Lord in her heart. (She later concluded that she had not before been saved.)

She was so thrilled that she began immediately testifying to her friends and led another church member, a senior in high school, into the same rejoicing.

A day or two later, it came her turn in class at school to relate some personal experience. She told of the special meetings at her church and joyfully described her new experience in the Lord.

By the time her friend had done the same, another friend burst out weeping, and said, "I am a member of that church but have never known the Lord!" The teacher was perturbed indeed. The pastor's daughter relieved the situation by exclaiming, "Let me take her to my daddy!" The three were excused for the remainder of the afternoon.

I reached their home just in time for the rejoicing. What a thrill to see and hear their joy!

The red-hot testimony of the two daughters of the pastor moved the married daughters. One discovered at the time that she had not been saved, and later on the other had the same experience of being made over.

Some time after I came home, the lovely mother learned what it really means to assign the old self to death and so enthrone Christ that the Holy Spirit could fill. Precious was the letter telling me about it!

While there, I occupied a room in the basement apartment in the pastor's home, but went to the church for all personal interviews. On Friday a deacon telephoned that he wanted to see me at six P.M., his last chance, not at the church but at the pastor's home. We sat on the sofa in the little apartment living room, as he told me that his greatest problem was smoking. For thirty-four years he had tried to quit and could not. He was a deacon and did not think that a deacon should smoke. But in spite of all of his praying about it, he had not been able to quit.

When I asked if he had faced up to his sins and listed them, he replied that he had written down thirty-four. My suggestion was that perhaps the reason that the Lord had not been able to deliver him from smoking was that he had been trying to quit by himself "with" the Lord's help—as if he himself could almost make it, but just needed a little assistance. I had seen people by scores try it that way, only to fail. I knew that if he ever were delivered that he would have to admit to the Lord that he was a slave and could not quit, that unless the Lord delivered him he would have to go on in bondage for life.

I also suggested that perhaps it was because he had too many other sins in his life to separate him from the Lord to get his prayer answered, and that the best start would be to get on his knees and transfer all the sins that he could think of in his life over to the Lord Jesus Christ, thanking him that he already had taken the punishment for those sins. I told him that I would not listen.

I moved a distance away. On our knees he poured out his sins one by one while I prayed for him in an undertone. However, sometimes he was so convicted and heartsick that he confessed them in such loud tones that I could not help but hear. Little did he care by that time! With weeping, the last he confessed was having had too much to do with women.

After a time of confession, he said, "I wish I had my list here, I am afraid I will forget some of my sins!" He then transferred to the Lord any on the list that he had not recalled and all that he had forgotten to list since he was saved. When they were blotted out one by one and up-to-date, I asked what kind of nature produced all of those sins. His quick response was, "a black sinful nature." He then put himself over on the cross, thanking the Lord that he not only took all of his sins to the cross but took him there, and had been seeing him in that position ever since he was saved.

By a definite act of his will he told the Lord that he was through with the old self. When we had read such passages as Psalm 103:12 and Micah 7:19, he was ready to live that Christ might be enthroned in his heart, and to show only him through his personality. We invited the Holy Spirit, whose work it is to keep him in the place of death and magnify Christ, to take over and literally fill him up! (The smoking habit of 34 years had not been mentioned.)

With rejoicing he rushed off to the church! When I arose to speak he said, "Miss Bertha, I want to give a testimony." The man who had not wanted anyone to know that he was going to see me began by saying, "I had a time of prayer with Miss Bertha before the service." He ended his testimony by saying, "The Lord has delivered me from thirty-four years of smoking!"

Funeral Shout

A Christian Life Conference in 1971, held at Graham Heights Church in Memphis, Tennessee, drew many from other churches. The invitation was given for any who were ready to assign the old self to death, and *will* that Christ should be magnified in their hearts and lives instead of the "big I." One handsome woman came first. Soon, so many women had come that the pastor had to take the men into another room for prayer help.

When I knelt beside that first woman, she said, "For thirty-eight years I have done everything that a woman can do in a Baptist church or association. I have gotten nowhere with all of my study and efforts. I am absolutely sick of all my Christian work."

I explained to her that the Lord's plan calls for our old selves to take the place of death, then for us to dedicate our cleansed personalities to him. We are to will that only Christ shall be enthroned. Then the Holy Spirit, who came into our hearts when we were saved, can take over and literally fill us and keep the old self in the place of death. As we will it so, he will keep Christ enthroned. We can say with Paul, "I live; yet not I, but Christ liveth in me." We thus become the Lord's wealth.

First, the woman transferred every known sin to the Lord Jesus Christ, thanking him that he took it all in his own body to the cross. She then was instructed to transfer that sinful self to him, since he not only took all that the sinful self produced, but took her every human nature to the cross.

When she had thanked him for this and plunged into the blood of Jesus for cleansing from all that the old devil nature had contaminated, she told the Lord that it was now her will that only her Lord Jesus Christ should be magnified in her body.

Her heart was then prepared for the Holy Spirit to fill her. Praise the Lord! She did not have to tarry ten days for the Holy Spirit to come down from heaven. He had come into her heart when she was saved. But she, not knowing that she should "move out" as it were and give him all of the space, had dwelt there herself. She had been filled with herself *and* with the Holy Spirit. Sometimes more of self, and sometimes less of self, but always self was there. Thus the Holy Spirit grieved and was pushed back, even though he patiently did the very best he could for her.

Being filled with the Holy Spirit means that he is the only personality there!

When she became so sick of her old self that she made a complete break with it, and willed henceforth to live dead to self with Christ enthroned, the Holy Spirit took over and literally filled up all of the space. He would keep her where she had willed herself to live and magnify Christ because she *willed* that.

That dear woman was so thrilled when the transaction had been made that she started saying, "Praise the Lord! Praise the Lord!" And in a moment she was up praising the Lord.

She was tall, beautifully dressed, and looking the picture of elegance with her mink cape. She walked to and fro saying, "Hallelujah! Hallelujah! Praise the Lord! Praise the Lord! Praise the Lord! Hallelujah!"

The joy of the Lord so filled my own soul that I started laughing. The room was full of other women who were having an object lesson in what the Lord had in store for them. It all so filled my soul that the more she shouted the more I laughed, and the more I laughed the more she shouted. The climax was reached when she exclaimed, "Who ever thought that I would shout at my own funeral!"

I later learned that she was a cousin to the missionary, Miss Pearl Caldwell, who labored so effectively among the 35 churches in Pingtu county preparing the way for the part they had in the glorious Shantung Revival.

Confessed Sin

"Filled with all the fullness of God" (Eph. 3:19).

When the Crusade of the Americas was being set up, I was asked to go help prepare the pastors in Phoenix, Arizona. Fifty-six pastors, with some from the state Baptist office, went out thirty miles from the city into the hills to a motel called Wrangler's Roost, which could take care of just that many. All went prepared to stay for two and a half days.

Thursday morning we started in with a message on "The Power of Prayer," followed by one on "Sin Hindering Prayer." By noon they had heard enough on sin to respond to my suggestion that each go away for awhile before lunch and make a list of every sin in their hearts and lives, numbering each one. This was to be secret between self and the Lord.

In the afternoon we had more messages on the tragedy of sin in a Christian. We only set time for opening sessions and took breaks as we needed them. At each break, men were sent out to meet with the Lord alone. They asked him to show any sins of which they were unconscious. Some were amazed at the number the Lord showed them.

Burying People Alive

One day we talked of the danger in crusades of letting people make false professions, and "deciding for Christ" without miracles taking place in their hearts. The group was so interested that we took some time talking about what it means to be born of the Spirit.

Among the points discussed was that there can be no salvation apart from repentance. When one is on the broad way that leads to hell, he cannot get into that narrow way without doing his part. He must see his danger, turn around, come to the foot of the cross, make a definite break with sin, transfer his sins and his sinful self to Christ, and take Christ's death for everything that he is that is unlike Holy God. Jesus sent people out to preach repentance toward God and faith in the Lord Jesus Christ. The death of Christ can mean nothing to a person who is unconscious of being a sinner. Even little children can be just as heavily convicted of sin as a grown person, just as I was when ten years old.

We further discussed the fact that it is not *our* faith

which saves us. Saving faith is imparted by the Holy Spirit, or we do not have it! When does the Holy Spirit impart saving faith? When we change our attitudes toward sin and self. If we go through the form of baptizing people who do not know that they are sinners against Holy God, repent of that sin, meet Christ at the cross to take refuge in his death from what they are by nature and, because of this step, receive a living Lord in their hearts, we baptize people who have not died in Christ.

I also told the pastors that I had never known but two classes of people who bury folk who are still alive. Many years ago a rich landowner in China had a grave dug the size of a living room on his estate, and all that he had used in life was buried with him to use in the next life. Bed, basin, tables, writing materials, books, teapots, cups, stools, chairs, and a live slave were buried with him to serve him in the next world.

This heathen practice was discontinued long ago.

The second class of people who bury live folk are preachers who baptize unsaved people—people who have never come to the cross and entered into Christ's death, thus dying in him. At our retreat in the prayer time afterwards, one pastor wailed out, "Lord, forgive me for burying live people!"

The Big I

The next lesson was a leaflet which I formerly secured from Scotland, called, "Not I But Christ." A big athlete is standing up tall at the top of the page, and at the bottom he is on his knees in the big letter "C" of Christ. The whole message of the leaflet is a list of sins of the heart. When each had gone away alone to underscore each sin listed that applied to him personally, they said that they had to underscore the whole list.

By time for the evening break, they were ready to go alone with the Lord, get on their knees, and get that sin list settled up. How did they settle it? Praise the Lord, there was "a fountain opened in the house of David . . . for sin and uncleanness" (Zech. 13:1).

They put the first sin over on Christ and thanked him that he had taken that sin in his own body when he went to the cross. (Isa. 53). Thus the sin was transferred to Christ. They knew that if they were saved sin would not send them to hell, but anything unclean would grieve the Holy Spirit and break fellowship with the Lord in this life, as well as cause him to suffer loss in heaven. That sin then was no longer on them, but on the Lord. If that sin, number one, was just between the offender and the Lord, with no other human being involved, it could then be marked off the list, and the Lord's promise claimed that he will forget that the person was ever guilty of that sin (Isa. 43:25).

Sin number two may have involved some other individual as well as the Lord. That sin was transferred to the cross of Christ, in the same way as number one, but it could not be marked from the list until that person was contacted not only with the proper apology, but restitution made if necessary. When the prayer retreat members had gone through the whole sin list in that way, they were halfway ready to pray.

We next started on the "Big I" in all of us. We had a half day's teaching on the trouble that this sinful human nature causes, the sin principle which we inherited from fallen Adam and Eve—what it does and what its symptoms are.

When I had finished a message along this line, one of the state workers arose and said, "Brethren, what this woman is teaching us is total depravity; we do not hear much about this nowadays!" However, everyone continued to listen most carefully and cooperated in every suggestion made.

By Friday afternoon they were ready to get on their knees and one by one dethrone that "Big I," so that the Holy Spirit might fill and be the power in them which they wanted. As they did this, they told the Lord audibly that they were agreeing with him and that he had put the heredity of sin in them in the place of death, where it belonged when they identified with Christ in his death to be saved. Not knowing that, they had been trying to crucify themselves; now they were ready to cooperate with the Lord and assign the old self to its rightful place: "*death*."

One by one, they had a transaction with the Lord; speaking aloud. They told the Lord that they were at that time choosing Christ to reign in them and in every situation in their lives.

Next, they thanked the Lord that the "Big I," which had been in the place of death in God's sight since they were saved, had become so in their own sights because they had chosen that place for themselves.

This prepared the way for the Holy Spirit, who had been in their hearts since the day that they were saved, to come out of that grieved and quenched corner and take over and fill up all of the space which had been left. They reminded the Lord that what they were asking was his will and plan for them, and now it was their own will. Since man's will and God's will had come together, all the devils in hell could not keep the Holy

Spirit from filling them!

As each one made this transaction with the Lord and settled his own filling, each started to pray for those who still struggled. One man who had been a missionary under the Home Mission Board with the Chinese and had been greatly used in his early years was having difficulty in his work. The Chinese had become cold. Worse still, the church had a rich man who was "church boss."

Needless to say, the missionary was completely discouraged and heartbroken over the situation. He kept begging the Lord to dethrone him, crying out, "Lord, crucify me! Lord, crucify me! I do not want anything to do with my old self any longer." All who had already entered their place in "the heavenlies" were praying for him, while the remainder of the group still was taken up with praying for themselves.

Finally the distressed man paused in his pleading, long enough for me to direct him with,"Brother! the Lord is not going to do that for you! Had he been going to crucify you, he would have done so long ago! In fact, he *did* crucify you in his Son. He will not force you over your will to accept that. The Lord never does anything for you over your will and choice. He has been waiting ever since you were saved for you to take this position for yourself. He is still waiting until you, by a definite act of your will, assign that old self to the position of death where the Lord already sees you!"

Instead of further pleas, a struggle began. The man tried again and again to tell the Lord that he was right then dethroning himself, but he just could not. While the rest of us resisted the devil and pled for the Lord to complete his miracle of deliverance, the poor seeker could only hum and haw until finally he surprised us all with the exclamation, "Lord, I lay this stinking carcass down!"

That evening we were on praying ground as a group! What a joy when people who come together to pray are of one accord and so cleansed and so dead to themselves that they can unitedly approach the throne of God and pray for his work for his own glory! Yes, they asked him to do that which he cannot do unless those who are right with him do ask!

We were there to pray for the coming crusade in Phoenix. Young James Robison, at that time twenty years old, a phenomenal evangelist of Texas, was to be the preacher. The eleven thousand seating capacity stadium had been rented.

We began at seven P.M. to pray for that crusade. Before we started, the question was asked, "Are all sins forgiven and confessed so that we can pray effectively?" Someone answered, "We have not seen our wives yet!" Yes, perhaps most of them would have to humble themselves and make confessions to their wives, but the Lord was seeing that as already done, since he knew that they were going to obey him.

First, we had a marvelous time praying for their wives, bringing each one as they were named and unitedly standing them up before the throne of God, asking him for his own glory to do in them what they needed.

Next we presented the evangelist, the singer, the choir, the committees, one by one to the Lord. I never heard of so many committees, but not one was left out.

We took our stand against the devil and claimed the Lord's protection against accidents in traffic. We asked for the amount of money that would be needed, and above all for the Holy Spirit to empower the speaker and pervade the atmosphere of the place that the devil would have no chance to snatch away the Word.

We asked that not one counselor would deceive any one into thinking that he was saved just because of a mental belief in Jesus, but that each unsaved one would be brought to the cross as a sinner, to repent and enter into Christ's death. We especially asked the Lord to save some of the eighty thousand Mormons in Phoenix.

There was no repetition in prayer as we named the objects and the leader presented them to the Lord in a few words. How long do you suppose that prayer lasted? From seven in the evening until eleven o'clock. No one had thought about time; we were all "in the heavenlies," so to speak, doing business with God (Eph. 2:7).

By noon Saturday all returned home. One young pastor usually spent Saturday afternoon with his family. However, on this Saturday afternoon he felt led to do something different. Even though he had been away from home since breakfast on Thursday, he felt led to go to his church nearby and have a time of prayer. As he walked along the street from his home, he passed a teen-age boy and asked, "Do you know Jesus Christ as your personal Savior?" The reply was, "No." "Has anyone ever told you how to be saved?" The boy answered again, with "No." The pastor then asked, "Would you like to know?" When the boy answered in the affirmative, he invited him into the church. After two hours the youngster went away rejoicing in his Savior.

On Sunday morning that pastor gave his experience of getting right with God, with apologies to the church for wasting time and preaching to them without being equipped with power to do so, and he told what the Lord had done for him because he dethroned the old self and let the Holy Spirit take over.

When he finished, he did not give the usual invitation, but said to the congregation, "If any of you want to be filled with the Holy Spirit, meet me here at the church this afternoon at 2:30."

Fourteen people were there. He carefully told them what would be required of them, and handed each a pencil and paper; then sent them off, each alone, to a Sunday School room to face up to their sins and list them. Some went home immediately, others later, but four stayed through to the dethroning of self and appropriating the Holy Spirit to take over and literally fill them.

What a change in the services of other pastors over the city! The crusade some weeks later proved to be beyond anything that the planning committee could have ever hoped. Personal workers had been so trained by the Spirit-filled and Spirit-guided T. D. Hall that they knew how to lead a person to the foot of the cross to meet the Savior. It was reported that more than two thousand lost souls, including some Mormons, were saved, and a thousand cold Christians brought back into fellowship with God, and some others were built up in their faith.

Later when I saw some of the pastors in New Orleans at the Southern Baptist Convention, they said, "The victory for that crusade was won at Wrangler's Roost in that prayer retreat."

Cooperating With God

The first day of a recent October, I went to Indianapolis at the call of the state WMU secretary to lead a statewide prayer retreat for members of the Woman's Missionary Union.

One hundred and forty women went to a camp several miles away. The first day we met under a pavillion. The weather was warm and beautiful. The precious hungry-hearted women were ready to do anything that I suggested, so all went away after the afternoon session and listed their sins.

That evening we talked about the old sinful nature, showing that trying to improve it is hopeless. Christ came to put it to death, and we have to do the same, by agreeing with him and assenting to it.

The second day there was such a wind that we had to crowd into the little chapel only half large enough for the group. Benches were too close together for us to kneel. I had led a prayer retreat sometime before for the Southern Baptist pastors in that state who had told the women of their churches that they had better carry a prayer cushion, for Miss Bertha would have them on their knees. The women sat on the cushions on the cement floor up and down the aisles and around the pulpit. The morning of that day was given to a discussion of the Holy Spirit's work in us, and the afternoon to prayer.

I felt sure that some were ready to dethrone *self* and so enthrone Christ that the Holy Spirit could fill them. I suggested that they one by one stand for public transaction with the Lord.

With all heads bowed, they began to stand two and three at a time, thanking the Lord that all of their sins had been laid on Christ and, according to his Word, they were washed white as snow. The old self had been assigned to death and Christ enthroned to reign.

They then invited the Holy Spirit to take over and fill. For nearly two hours they kept on without a moment lost. When I realized that the time to start home was near, I suggested that those who had not had a chance and wanted to stand, to lift their hands sincerely and silently pray the same prayer. Every hand but one of those who had not stood went up.

We had with us the widow of a missionary to China, now retired and living with her daughter in Indiana. She sat all day with the WMU secretary on a backless bench in the little foyer. With no cushion, she got on her knees on that cement floor and lifted her voice so that all could hear. She told the Lord that for thirty-five years she had longed and prayed to be filled with the Holy Spirit (from the time that she married and went to China).

She praised the Lord for what she had heard those days, and thanked him that her sins were all forgiven up-to-date, and at that moment she was dethroning herself and making Christ King of kings in her heart and life and was choosing that and willing it, and she knew that the Holy Spirit would make this actually true. She then asked the Holy Spirit to fill her and praised him for doing so.

After about ten days, I began to receive letters from the women. One wrote that when she began to list her sins and ask the Lord to reveal more to her, he showed her that she was nothing but sin, and not fit for anything but hell. About 95 percent of her conversation she now saw was useless and the world could get along just as well without it. She was made absolutely sick of her constant chatter, chatter!

She cried to the Lord for deliverance from her tongue. Driving home, she prayed and praised the Lord for the peace and joy in her soul and for the wonderful cleansing which had come. She then asked herself, "How can I continue like this? I cannot stand to go back to that old life of empty, incessant talk. Lord, how can I so cooperate with you that I can remain delivered from that terrible habit?"

She wrote that the Lord told her to stop at the first drugstore and buy a roll of adhesive tape and seal up her lips. She just obeyed. With her lips all stuck together, she went driving along. Then she said to herself, "This will not do! My husband will think that I have had a wreck." She pulled over to the side of the highway and wrote a note to the husband telling him that the Lord had been dealing with her and had convicted her of so much talk, that from now on she would cooperate with God and keep quiet for a few days. I am sure the husband thanked the Lord for that prayer retreat! He went in and told the children that their mother wanted to keep quiet with the Lord for a few days; perhaps she would explain to them why later on. They agreed to do their best to cooperate and get along without her having to talk.

In the letter, she wrote that she never dreamed that one could get along so well without talking! She removed the tape only to eat and did that in silence—I believe for seven days. On the eighth day, when she was at home alone, the Holy Spirit, whom she had "faithed" to fill her at the retreat, let her know that he literally had taken over. She began to bear the fruit of such joy that she shouted all over the house. By the ninth day, the husband too had been filled and was rejoicing in the same way.

Sharing With the Congregation

In September, 1972, I attended a pastor's prayer retreat at Reidville, North Carolina. Roy Hoover told me that he had been filled with the Holy Spirit three months before and everything had been different since. One day, when praying during the retreat, he thanked the Lord for having led him to get all of his sins forgiven up-to-date and taking the place of death to himself, for the fact that Christ was enthroned in his heart, and that the Holy Spirit was filling him and making all of the above real. What else could he ask the Lord to do for him? But he did have a good request to make of the Lord. At the close of his prayer of thanksgiving he said, "Now, Lord, just keep me right where I am at! But there was something which he had not done. The last day of the retreat I suggested that they each go to their homes and first share with their wives and make any apologies necessary. I then suggested that the next Sunday they tell their churches what the Lord had done, and each make any confessions needed to the church. I added that in every case where a pastor and his wife had gone all the way with the Lord, and had shared this with their congregation, that a revival had followed.

Not by just announcing that they had been blessed at the retreat (people do not know how to be blessed), but in an honest and humble way relate just the steps that had been taken: They had faced up to sins and listed them in order that they might not omit any which needed to be made right with others. Then, they put the old self with their sins on the cross. (The Lord had put their sins and the old self there when they were saved.) Then, by faith, they put Christ upon the throne of their hearts to be their absolute monarch; they "faithed" the Holy Spirit to take over and fill their souls. In every group there are a few who are heart-hungry, just wanting to know how to get that hunger satisfied.

From the following letter you will see what took lace in Brother Hoover's church:

DEAR MISS BERTHA,

Just a note to thank you for sharing with us your knowledge of the Word at the prayer retreat at Camp Van recently. His ways are marvelous to behold! On Sunday after the retreat, I gave my testimony of what the Lord had done for me over the last three months, including what he did for me during the retreat.

I left the pulpit without an invitation, just told the folks if they wanted something different that I would be in the study. I was not able to leave until 3:00 P.M.

Revival has come to my home. My wife has been filled with the Spirit gloriously! She even gave up her job of full-time work. People are calling me, wanting to be saved. Christians are disturbed; some are getting right. Others are so miserable that they do not know what to do. The past Wednesday evening we had prayer instead of Bible study. I have never felt the presence of God any more anywhere. I could write a book over what the Lord has already done here. Many have said, "Roy Hoover has gone off the deep end!" People sure are wondering what has taken place.

We are still praying for you and your eyes and your sister. Do remember me that the Lord will keep me "dead," and that I will be submissive to his will at all times! Love and best wishes to you because of him.

ROY HOOVER

Church Parlor Becomes Prayer Room

Such a hunger has the Lord put into the hearts of his own to know him better that I receive enough invitations ahead to keep me rushing for four or five years.

One of our pastors wrote to ask me for a week at his church. Not knowing him and not supposing that either he or the church were ready for my type of message, I just replied that I could not accept.

The next year he wrote again, only to be turned down. After another year, he called me to urge that I go, and informed me that he had been in one of the classes at Southwestern Seminary where I had spoken. Even though he was able to hear only one message, it resulted in his going to his room, getting on his knees with his Bible open, and giving himself such a going over that he never had been the same.

Seeing that the man knew what he was doing by inviting me to his church, I promised him the very first week that I could arrange. In a few months, I was there.

What hunger on the part of the pastor, staff, and other church leaders I found! They cooperated beautifully in facing up to sins first, and then self, and soon were ready to do what had to be done about both.

They had just done some overhauling of the church, and made a big ladie's parlor in back of the auditorium.

That ladies' parlor was divided into two parts, with an accordian partition easily closed, just made for a prayer room. If anyone wanted to get married in it, they could be married in the prayer room. They need not do anything in a church parlor that they could not do in a room for prayer.

I started in as usual with my three services on Sunday, asking for Sunday afternoon homework—the listing of sins. They cooperated.

Monday, the pastor told me of a prayer group of eight men who met every Tuesday morning from 6:00 to 6:50 to pray with him, and asked if they could come over to the motel and have me join them. Of course, that was my special joy. I had learned how to receive men in my room, whether one or in groups, by just pulling back the front curtains. No one can be arrested in the United States for being seen on his knees praying, even with a woman!

I had also learned what Hollywood beds were made for—to kneel around. We all knelt around with a thick carpet under our knees, and a softness for our elbows, so no one was tempted to think of his human body.

The pastor and his music director were so hungry-hearted that, having placed their sins on the cross of Christ, they were ready to deal with old human nature and assign it to death. They then willed Christ on the throne of their hearts and lives, and faithed the Holy Spirit to take over and fill!

They asked if they could return each morning. The next morning a few more reached the position before the Lord of being filled, and went away rejoicing.

They even came Saturday, though they did not have to get up early and go to work. But since I did not have to leave for the plane until 9:00 o'clock, I was happy for one more blessed chance of uniting my heart with those who were on praying ground.

One morning a young layman, who is a university graduate though not always sounding like it when he spoke, said in his prayer, "Lord, how I do thank you for cleansing me from all of my sins, delivering me from the old self, and filling my soul! The Bible has become a new book; last night when I read the eighth chapter of Romans, I nearly busted!"

The wife of the music director had been nine years in that church seeing another member graciously look after an afflicted son—day after day, week after week, month after month, and year after year with no hope of ever an improvement.

Yet that woman with other members of her family went right on: present at church services, active in Sunday School, WMU, Training Union, looking after her home, and in everything showing Christ expressing himself through her.

The music director's wife, with never a burden except her sinful self, was hungry for what she saw in that mother. She just knew that Martha knew the Lord in a way that she did not, and that was just what she wanted. Month by month the hunger grew stronger.

In the autumn of that year she went with her husband to the State Convention which was held in a town on the coast of South Georgia. She was so sick of herself and so longed for something better that one day during the Convention she went out on the beach and sat for three hours alone, just crying to the Lord for him to do something new in her.

Not knowing how to let him do what she wanted, she returned more hungry-hearted than ever.

She was church secretary for another nearby church, but on Thursday worked only in the forenoon. She asked that I go to her home for lunch on that day.

Often when busy women invite me to lunch I ask, "Do you have religion enough to serve me a glass of milk and a sandwich? If so, I will accept. If you are so proud in your heart that you want to prepare a big meal, I will not accept. Special meeting times at church are not the times for big meals!"

I was happy to find that she had that much religion! She arrived from her work just as the husband and I reached her home, bringing in her hand a pie from the baker's shop, which she had passed. She opened the oven and took out a cake of warm cornbread and set out the milk. Who from South Carolina or Georgia could have wanted more? She was really too miserable for much conversation, except to tell why she so wanted me to come.

As soon as we finished eating, we went to the den and got on our knees by the sofa. It took no persuading for her to empty out her burdened soul to the Lord. She already had listed and confessed every sin that she knew about, and all that the Holy Spirit had revealed to her that week as she compared herself with the Lord's holy standard.

That precious woman wept until she could hardly weep more, not thinking or caring how she looked. The husband, you will recall, had been filled Tuesday morning at the small group prayer meeting. He on one side of her and I on the other took turns, in the authority of the Lord Jesus Christ, rebuking the devil and pleading with the Lord to complete his work in her heart.

When I saw that there were really no more ways in which she could die to herself, to all the emptiness of life and even to all the good things in life, I started reading God's promises to her.

She began thanking the Lord that because she had assigned the old self to death that she was dead. God had her in that position since she had been saved, now she could thank the Lord that once and for all she was through with herself. Good riddance!

She already had willed the Lord on the throne of her heart, so she just as readily thanked him that the Holy Spirit would enthrone Christ as her Lord and King.

Being told that her heart was now ready for the Holy Spirit to take over and fill up, since it was his will and her will, she invited him to do so. From the Word of God, she saw that when we ask anything according to his will, "He heareth us" and "we know that we have the petitions that we desired of him" (John 5:14-15).

When she asked the Holy Spirit to take over and fill her, he did so, and her first exclamation was, "He has been there all the time, I just didn't know it!" What a testimony she has had since.

By midweek the ladies' parlor had become two prayer rooms after each session—one for those wanting the Holy Spirit to fill them and needing prayer, help, and guidance; and the other for those not needed otherwise to unite their cleansed, filled hearts in prayer for the other roomful. How the Holy Spirit worked!

Sunday morning the pastor and music director gave their testimonies to the Holy Spirit's filling.

The plan for Sunday evening was to give all who had been blessed during the week a chance to tell what the Lord had done for them. When only a few had spoken, hungry-hearted people stood all over the church and poured out their requests for spiritual help.

Useless saved people wanted something more. Church members wanted a "know so" salvation. Defeated Christians wanted victory in their daily lives, and the unsaved wanted the Savior. The pastor gave them two hours, without realizing the time.

And on it went, Sunday after Sunday, with the atmosphere of church services completely changed.

PART THREE

Messages Which the Lord Has Used

4

SELF-DEDICATED MOSES

Moses no doubt had learned from this mother that God was to lead Israel back to Canaan and give the land to them. (Children in the East have a nurse until they are in school, and sometimes even afterwards.) His mother nurse had time to instill much into his heart, and she probably remained in the court as a maid. At any rate, there was something there for the Lord to use to call him to lead God's people out of Egypt.

He gave up life with all its pleasures and its luxuries and the glories of Egyptian court life, and went out to identify himself with a race of slaves.

Moses is a classic example of one dedicating old self to the Lord to do a job for him. He gave up all this, and of course he thought that all that Israel would need was a leader. If he were willing to give up so much to become their leader, certainly they would cooperate.

One day he went out and saw an Egyptian taskmaster smite one of his brethren. He looked this way and that way, and when he was sure no one would see him, instead of looking up and asking, "Lord, is this the way you want it done?" he used his strong right arm and killed the Egyptian and hid him in the sand. Did he go home rejoicing over his victory? (One less Egyptian to oppress his people.) Did Moses go to bed that night pleased over the success of the day?

You remember that when he went out the next day he saw two Hebrews fighting. Moses went up to exhort the guilty one not to treat his brother so badly, but the guilty one resented the interference and accused Moses of killing the Egyptian the day before, even though Moses had done so for the sake of the Israelite!

Worse still, the news of Moses' consecrated effort reached Pharoah, and Moses—with all his good intentions—had to flee for his life. He did not feel safe until he got all the way into desert land in the vicinity of Mount Sinai.

For forty years, Moses—after all of his dedication to do a job for God—was in the desert following sheep. How his call from God must have puzzled him during those next forty years!

Stephen, in his sermon in Acts 7 describes Moses as being learned in all the wisdom of the Egyptians, and mighty in word and deed.

The result of Moses' self-consecrated working for God was that he spent forty years of solitude in the desert doing that which men can do who do not know one letter in books from another, or have ever been ten miles from home.

The result to the Israelites of Moses' blunder was that another generation had to go on being oppressed by Egyptians and thousands no doubt beaten by cruel overseers. Another generation found graves in Egypt because Moses was unusable.

Year after year Moses lived in the desert with the sheep. His employer gave him his daughter for a wife, which must have been a great comfort to Moses. What thoughts must have gone through his mind as he walked through that sandy desert sagebrush. What remorse over having tried to deliver his people! How his call must have puzzled him during those forty years!

One day when God was sure that Moses had come to the end of himself and all that he himself could do to deliver Israel, the call came again. This time the call came from the burning bush. God said to him, "I am the God of thy father, the God of Abraham, the God of Isaac, and the God of Jacob. I have surely seen the affliction of my people which are in Egypt, and I have heard their cry by reason of their taskmasters; for I know their sorrows; and I am come down to deliver them out of the hand of the Egyptians, and to bring them into Canaan" (Ex. 3:6-8a).

But God had not been able to accomplish that deliverance because the only one whose life he had spared as a baby for the purpose—the only one whom he had put in a position to be educated and prepared—had gone out on his own to use his own methods to meet the situation. Now the Lord, after forty years, had this man ready! Moses would not deliver them, but Jehovah God would.

"Come now therefore, and I will send thee unto Pharoah, that thou mayest bring forth my people, the children of Israel out of Egypt" (v. 10). Moses hid his face in fear at God's introduction of himself. His reply was, "Who am I, that I should go unto Pharoah, and that I should lead the children of Israel out of Egypt?"

(v. 11). As if Jehovah God did not know what he was doing.

All of the Lord's work has been turned over to his children. If they do not cooperate with him so that he can do it through them, it must go undone. Moses had been in Jehovah God's desert school for forty years following sheep, and now God called again and Moses feared. No wonder, after his miserable failure the first time! One thing sure, he would never dedicate self to go out to do a job for God again! He had come to the very end of Moses.

Exodus 4:2 says, "What is that in thine hand?" Moses replied, "A rod" (the sign or badge of a shepherd). "Take this rod in thine hand" (v. 17). And Moses realized he was going before Pharoah with nothing but a rod—as if to say, I am nothing but a shepherd.

Moses had excuses, but the Lord won out in spite of them. When Moses was willing to go, having become nothing but a shepherd, the Lord's opportunity had come. The rod became the Lord's rod, and how he used it! Yes, how he used Moses and the rod to secure the release of Israel!

The mighty present-tense God would do just what he had said that he would. With the rod stretched out, the waters of the Red Sea divided. With the rod again stretched out, the waters closed on the Egyptian army. With the rod, he stretched up toward God in trust to him for victory, and the Amalekites were defeated. Moses had taken his orders from Jehovah God!

God took them out across every hindrance, all through the forty years wandering in the wilderness, right up to the border of the land, because his leader was nothing but a shepherd.

5

GEHAZI: THE HIGH COST
OF LOW MOTIVES

Second Kings 5 contains some interesting and valuable history for us. Naaman, the highest military official, who stood next to the King in the court of the enemy to the north of Israel, was a leper. Through a captive from Israel who resided in his home, he heard of a man down in Israel who could cure leprosy.

His king gave him a leave of absence and sent him off with quite a military escort. Arriving at the court in Samaria, Naaman presented the letter of introduction and request from his king to the king of Israel.

The king of Israel, thinking that the Syrian king was trying to find some excuse for invading Israel, rent his garments and exclaimed, "Who can cure leprosy but God?"

God had his prophet in Israel, named Elisha. When he heard of the situation, he sent a message to the king: "Send that man to me and he will know that there is a prophet in Israel."

Naaman and his party—quite a number in their war chariots—all went down to the humble cottage of Elisha. Elisha knew the pride of that heathen captain, and he knew that Naaman would have to become humble before Holy God could meet him. The prophet helped the Lord out by not even going out to meet the great man. He just sent his servant, Gehazi, out to advise the great man that Elisha had said to go down to the river Jordan and dip seven times, with the promise that if he did so he would be healed.

Such a reception, or lack of reception, in the East was unthinkable. According to all custom, Elisha should have been outside the gate and even out in the street to start bowing when Naaman came in sight.

Naaman was angered beyond words at not being received! He was ready to go back to Damascus, and would have, had not his officials under him and his accompanying bodyguard pled with him to go do what had been suggested.

Finally, Naaman humbled himself and went down and dipped seven times and was perfectly cured.

After the way he had been treated by Elisha, he could have gone up the Jordan to the first ford, crossed over, and gone on back to Damascus. However, he was so grateful that he went up the hill, with all his company, to the home of Elisha, and had all the presents unloaded which he had brought down: ten talents of silver, six thousand pieces of gold, and ten changes of raiment. They would not have been ordinary men's suits as are worn today. No doubt the outer garments were gorgeous robes beaded with jewels.

Elisha had a seminary of one hundred students who sometimes had no food. Had Elisha lived today he would no doubt have exclaimed, "See how the Lord has provided!" His seminary would have been so endowed that never again would students have had to go out into the fields to gather a few greens to make soup!

Elisha would not accept one thing! When Naaman pled with him, Elisha's reply was, "As the Lord liveth, before whom I stand, I will receive none." Elisha ordered his life before his God, and was not going to let that heathen think that he was serving God for anything which he himself might get out of it. Hurrah for Elisha!

Verse 20 begins with, "But Gehazi." Something very different was coming. Yes, Gehazi, the servant of the man of God, stood there and SAW all of that wealth loaded up to be carried back to Damascus.

Secondly, he LUSTED after it; then, thirdly, he decided that he was going to have some of it. Fourthly, he stepped down from that high place of being associated with the Lord's prophet and went running after some of what that heathen man had. Poor, poor Gehazi! He sinned first with his *eyes,* then with his *heart,* then with his *mind* and *will.*

He stepped down from the highest position of any man in all of Israel, that of being a co-worker of the great man of God!

It was not safe for a man to travel alone in those days, and Elisha had left what family he had when he was called to be the Lord's prophet. Gehazi had traveled with him, eaten with him, prayed with him, and had taken the place of family. They had shared the little room on top of the wall at the Shunamite's home. In fact, it had been Gehazi who had suggested that the hostess be rewarded a son for her kindness. He saw that son grow large enough to follow his father to the field where, evidently, he suffered a stroke and died. Gehazi saw that boy come back to life. He had the most blessed position of any man in Israel, that of being associated with God's great prophet. How Elisha must have loved him!

As Gehazi went running after the chariots of Damascus, he immediately found a clever ally in the devil, to put into his mind just what to say to Naaman. When Naaman knew that he was coming, he stopped his chariot, got out and called back, "Is all well?" The answer was a lie from Gehazi's lips, "All is well." How could all be well when he had sold himself to the devil? Then another lie, "My master hath sent me" (vv. 21-22). Then another, "Two new seminary students have come, just arrived since you left. They are from Ephraim, a mountainous section where people are poor and could not go away to school." And next, "They are prophets' sons and need help. Give them, I pray, a talent of silver and two changes of raiment."

Grateful Naaman would have given him all that he had if he had asked for it. He did insist that they take two talents of silver. Naaman waited there by the side of the road while he sent two soldiers back with Gehazi to carry the silver and clothes.

Gehazi's plan had worked just beautifully. He had gotten more than he expected or could manage—often true of sin for a season!

As Naaman sat by the road and waited for the men to carry Gehazi's new wealth, Gehazi's mind must have soared. (The name "Gehazi" means visions.) From what follows, we see he lived up to his name.

As he saw the olive orchards he must have said, "I can have olive orchards with olive oil to sell." Passing the vineyards he said, "I can have vineyards and vine dressers, with wine and raisins for sale." At the sight of the sheep and shepherds on the hills, perhaps across the Jordan, and the herds of cattle in the meadows of the Jordan with the herdsmen, he exclaimed, "I can possess sheep, cattle, and servants!"

Eastern towns and cities at that time had towers outside the walls where watchmen looked out for the enemy in time of war. That was a time of peace and the tower was empty. Gehazi hid his loot in the house at the base of the tower and sent the two soldiers back to join Naaman.

What did that spiritually stupid Gehazi do after all of that sin? He went walking back to Elisha and reported for duty. Sin is so blinding that it makes men do unreasonable things. He did not know any better than to think that with all of the sin covered he could go on serving Elisha in the same way.

"But God . . ." How gracious was the Lord to his faithful prophet to save him from the tragedy of having a co-worker with hidden sin in his heart and life! He had revealed the whole thing to Elisha, everything that Gehazi had done and thought.

He asked, "Where did you come from, Gehazi?" Reply: "I have not been there!" (Another lie is added to all of his sins.)

(Here, I talk to the preachers and WMU leaders about sinning and going on back to church as usual, leading in prayer or preaching with sin separating them from Holy God. Sin always separates from God! I ask those present if they break the speed limit, which is breaking the law of the land and, therefore, becoming a criminal, and then go to the pulpit to preach. Who wants a criminal preaching to them? Who wants to hear a criminal leading in prayer? All kinds of so-called little sins may separate us from Holy God.)

Now look at the end of that sinning, lying hypocrite, Gehazi. Elisha must have loved Gehazi. But he could not keep such a co-worker.

Elisha had to say to him, "Is it a time to accept money and garments, olive orchards and vineyards, sheep and oxen, menservants and maidservants? Therefore the leprosy of Naaman shall cleave to you, and to your descendants forever." So Gehazi went out from the presence of Elisha a leper, as white as snow (2 Kings 5:26-27).

Poor Gehazi!

God's law forbade lepers to mingle with others. Every leper was quarantined to live outside the city or town, and it was God's law that if they saw anyone approach they had to call out, "Unclean! Unclean!" meaning, "I am a leper, do not come near me!"

Gehazi had come to that!

Oh, preacher, reader, beware of letting the devil tempt you with love of money, things, and ease! Stand straight before the Lord! You too are human, and that old self will never improve. It must be put in that position of death and kept there! The Lord is your inheritance!

6

CHRIST ENTHRONED

"For to me to live is Christ" (Phil. 1:21).

God's provision for holy living is Christ enthroned. Positively! The holy life is not our living, it is Christ so freely dwelling at ease in us that he actually can live his life through our personalities.

We rejoice over Colossians 1:27: "Christ in you, the hope of glory." Christ is in every believer, but that does not mean that all believers are living holy lives. Many are completely defeated. Why? Because the Christ in us does not force himself over our wills to do anything for us. He waits for us to will that he shall control us. Holy living presupposes death to self—our constantly choosing that position for the old sinful nature. This is necessary before we enthrone Christ. Living in that position is necessary for holy living. We are never holy if we rebel against Holy God. When we permit the old self to rise up and express itself, or even want to, we grieve the One who wants to live his holiness out in us and through us.

Colossians 3: 1-4: ". . . When Christ, who is our life, shall appear. . . ." Philippians 1:21: "For to me to live is Christ." It is Christ enthroned in the heart and life.

Since he lived thus in Paul, he also can live enthroned in you and me, and enable us to say, "I am crucified with Christ: nevertheless I live; yet not I, but Christ liveth in me" (Gal. 2:20).

What kind of life does Christ live in us? A life that is always victorious! That is always at peace and rest! That is equal to any situation which man or the devil and his demons may create!

This is what he wants to do for us.

When experiencing the wars of North China, I learned to pray in every situation, "Now, Lord, you are equal to this!" And he always was!

The secret is not to try to follow his example in our own strength, even with his help. He has something far better for his children than that!

He means for us to "rejoice" always, and "in every thing give thanks!" (1 Thess. 5:16,18).

Would a God of love make such heavy demands for us to carry out that they would be a constant burden? No, never! He is in us all that he demands of us. Yes, even to loving our enemies and praying for those who persecute us. (Matt. 5:44).

You may say this is not natural! Whoever thought that the Christian life is natural? The Christian life is supernatural. It is God's life in us!

Seven times Jehovah God pealed forth from Mount Sinai to Israel, "Be ye holy for I am holy," because he was to live in their midst. How else can we show our Lord to the lost world? We may *tell* a lot, but unless what we say is *shown* in our daily living, and in every emergency, our teaching will fail.

I heard a few years ago of a woman in Chicago who prayed for her sick husband thus: "Lord, I cannot stand to be left alone in the world with these two children to rear alone! I cannot be willing for you to take my husband." The husband continued to grow weaker. After a few days she prayed, "Lord, I cannot become willing for you to take him, but you are living in me. I trust you to be willingness in me!"

The husband died. The Lord was to her all that she needed as she started life over, being both mother and father to the children. However, she knew that it was not she who was getting along so well, but her Lord and Savior just expressing himself through her.

After a time, the mother was in the hospital, deathly ill. She cried to her Lord, "Oh, my loving Lord, I cannot be willing to die, and leave my children in the world with neither father nor mother! Spare me for their sakes, if it can be thy will!"

The next visit of the doctor brought the sad news that she had only a very short time left.

Again she prayed, "Lord, I cannot be willing to go and leave my children orphans in this sinful world, but they are yours. I turn them over to you and I ask you to be willingness in me to leave them."

In the Lord's glorious victory, she passed on.

7

HOW TO LET THE HOLY SPIRIT FILL

What does it mean to be filled?

When is a pitcher full of water? When there is nothing in it except water, and the water comes all the way to the top of the pitcher.

Suppose you have a pitcher of coffee and want a pitcher of water. If you empty half the coffee and fill up the pitcher with water, what do you have? A pitcher filled with coffee and water. If you leave one sip of the black liquid in the pitcher, you still have a pitcher of coffee and water. Only when you empty out all of the coffee and wash the pitcher can you have a pitcher full of clear water.

Most saved people are full of themselves and of the Holy Spirit. With some it is because they do not know that the Lord has anything better for them. Others, however, are unwilling to make the necessary break with their old selves and have only the Holy Spirit filling them. Still others are not filled because of ignorance of the teaching of the Word of God on the subject.

Since there is confusion on our relationship to Pentecost and on terminology used for the experience, it

seems necessary to take a look at Jehovah God's preparation for the baptism and the fullness of the Holy
Spirit.

When Jesus met his disciples in Jerusalem to be
taken up from them, he quoted the words of John the
Baptist (Acts 1:5), "Ye shall be baptized with the Holy
Ghost [Spirit] not many days hence."

You will recall that John baptized in water when
Jesus, who was to die the sinner's death, took the sinner's burial in the grave of water.

Jesus would bury them in the Holy Spirit. And Jesus
was filled with the Holy Spirit from birth. He said in
Luke 4:18, "The Spirit of the Lord is upon me, because he hath anointed me to preach the gospel to the
poor; he hath sent me to heal the brokenhearted, to
preach deliverance to the captives, and recovering of
sight to the blind, to set at liberty them that are
bruised, to preach the acceptable year of the Lord."

The disciples, believing what Jesus had said that
they would be baptized with the Holy Spirit, obeyed
the farewell injunction of the Lord and waited. They
spent the waiting time in prayer. Their praying did not
bring down the Holy Spirit. He could not have come
on any other day than had been set by Jehovah God.
Their praying no doubt prepared their hearts for his
coming.

Suddenly, they heard the sound, rushing and mighty!
It filled the room where they were sitting. When a
room is filled with wind, that means from floor to ceiling and from wall to wall. The one hundred and
twenty were all buried in the wind or baptized in the
Holy Spirit.

The group became one body, illustrated by Paul in 1

Corinthians 12 by the human body, each individual being a finger or toe or some member of the body, of which Christ is the head. A few times in the New Testament, this body is called "the church."

God's purpose was to dwell in the Temple in Jerusalem until his Son would come, but Israel so disobeyed God that he had to forsake them and permit them to be carried to Babylon to be chastened until they were cured of idol worship.

Ezekiel, in a vision, saw God's fire come out of the Temple and be escorted back to heaven by those four living creatures and their wheels, the purpose for which they had come down (Ezek. 9 to 11). God has never dwelt in buildings. He set a day when he would have living temples.

At Pentecost, the fire came back, a ball of fire which divided into one hundred and twenty flames and lit upon the head of each one.

Acts 2:4, states, "They were all filled with the Holy Ghost [Spirit]." Collectively, all were baptized into one. Individually, each received his or her own flame and each was filled. Here we see them all baptized with the Holy Spirit.

All were anointed with the Holy Spirit for what the Lord wanted of each; then all were filled. Each body became a temple.

Since Pentecost, every person baptized of the Holy Spirit is joined to the Body of Christ when saved, buried into Christ as described by our Lord in John 15, as a limb is joined to the tree. At the new birth, we are buried into him, thus we are in him and he in us, as Jesus said we would be (John 14:20).

No one after Pentecost ever was admonished to be

baptized with the Holy Spirit. No saved person in the New Testament after Pentecost is spoken of as having just been baptized with the Holy Spirit.

After Pentecost, the Word is used only in the following places, and each case refers to what took place when persons were saved. Romans 6:3: Ye who were baptized into Christ. 1 Corinthians 12:13: "By one Spirit are we all baptized into one body." Galatians 3:27: "As many of you as have been baptized into Christ have put on Christ." Colossians 2:12-13: "Buried with him in baptism, wherein also ye are risen with him through faith of the operation of God, who hath raised him from the dead. And you, being dead in your sins . . . hath he quickened [brought to life] together with him." Colossians 2:19-20: "Not holding the Head, from which all the body by joints and bands having nourishment ministered, and knit together. . . . Wherefore if ye be dead with Christ, . . . why . . . are ye subject to ordinances?" Colossians 3:1: "If ye be risen with Christ, seek those things which are above."

None of the above passages refer to water baptism, and all are past tense. Water baptism is but the outward confession to the world that we have been baptized into Christ, because we have entered into his death and died in him.

Another reference to being baptized by the Holy Spirit, after Acts 1:5, refers to the experience of being saved, Acts 11:16, where Peter reported to the Jerusalem Council on what God did for the household of Cornelius in Acts 10.

How may we be filled?

The Holy Spirit, remember, is holy. Anything from

the devil or from our sinful natures severs communion with him.

The first essential is to *deal with sins* committed since we were saved. There are just two places for our sins. They are either on us or they are on Christ. They are on us until we transfer them to Christ.

It is not enough to pray, "Lord, forgive my sins!" He does not have but one way to forgive sins. His only forgiveness is transferring those sins to the cross of his Son. When does he do that? When we do!

A good plan is to sit down with paper and pen and list them. There is a reason for this. Many of those sins are against other people. Some even have been forgotten, but Holy God has not forgotten any sin which has not been covered by the blood of Christ.

While sins will not send a saved person to hell, they will break fellowship with the Lord because they come from the devil.

When all sins that can be recalled are listed, it is good to pray the following prayer: "Lord, you are *light*. Shine into my heart and show me anything which should not be there!" If you are sincere, he will evermore bring to mind attitudes, thoughts, words, and deeds which you may not have diagnosed as sin. Many of these may have been against others. No one can be right with God and wrong with any person in the world.

How do we settle this sin account?

Look at sin number one. Whatever it is, transfer that sin to the Lord Jesus Christ, thanking him that he took all the punishment necessary for those sins. If that sin just involves you and the Lord, it can then be marked off, and the Lord, according to his Word, forgets that you were ever guilty of that sin (Jer. 31:34).

Sin number two may involve someone else. Place that sin on Christ and thank him that he bore it in his own body, but you cannot mark that sin off until you have made confession and, if necessary, restitution to the person.

When you have gone through all of your list in this way, you are ready to deal with the root of sin—self.

What can you do with self? First, what has God done about it? Christ not only took your sins to the cross, he took *you* there! He had to put you to death before he could have anything to do with you. No one can receive a living Lord into the sinful heart until the self has been put to death.

Only God can put us to death and leave us alive at the same time. God is too holy to associate with anything that comes from the devil. Therefore, he arranged that Christ should die in our stead. When we see our sinful selves and are ready to make a break with them and enter into Christ's death, God the Father charges the death of his Son to us, and sees us dead in Christ.

Dual government does not work. The "Big I" with its devil nature, when enthroned, forces the Holy Spirit into a corner of the heart.

We must dethrone it! Assign it to the place of death where the Lord has been seeing it since we were saved. When, by a definite act of your wills you take a positive stand against it, refusing in the name of the Lord to let it reign over you, the Lord takes the responsibility of making self ineffective over you.

Enthroning Christ

But the Lord does not force us to live in this position in which he sees us. By just the same way we may —by definite acts of our wills and of faith—enthrone Christ to rule instead of our old selves.

Since the work of the Holy Spirit is to magnify Christ, we are then, by an act of faith, to appropriate the Holy Spirit to come out of that crowded corner and fill us! He will fill up all of the space formerly occupied by self.

If he sees that we are clean, and that he is in complete possession of us, he will fill us just as he filled the tabernacle and the Jerusalem Temple when they were dedicated to him.

First, we know by faith that this has taken place, then we know it by experience.

Some Evidences of Being Filled

Christ becomes your very life—The fruit of the Holy Spirit listed in Galatians 5:22-23 are the characteristics of Christ. If Christ is being magnified through one's personality, that ninefold fruit of the Spirit is evident.

Courage—Another fruit of the Spirit is *courage.* This was one of the strongest characteristics of the apostles after Pentecost. "The righteous are bold as a lion" (Prov. 28:1).

Rest—"His rest shall be glorious" (Isa. 11:10). Rest of heart, rest of mind, resulting in rest of body, with complete relaxation, is indeed glorious!

Dr. Charles G. Trumbull, in his message to missionaries at North China Bible Conference, used the expression, "Lay Your Deadly Doing Down!" He referred to the efforts of missionaries trying to please God with their good works, thinking the more they did the better. Works had to be laid down because too much of it was in the energy of the flesh.

When missionaries learned to "let go and let God" instead of depending on their own efforts, the Holy Spirit could do his work through them. They rested while the work was going on.

One of the conference speakers used an illustration of stagecoach days, when an agent sold first-, second- and third-class tickets. When all were seated, a man with a first-class ticket asked the driver, "What is the use of my buying a first-class ticket when all of the seats are the same?" The driver replied, "You will find out later on." When they reached a muddy hill the driver called out, "All second-class ticket holders get out and walk." He next announced, "All third-class ticket holders get out and push." Then, "First-class ticket holders remain seated!"

The Spirit-filled person is guided in life and service. The psalmist said, in quoting the Lord, "I will guide thee with mine eye" (Ps. 32:8). Only one near enough to see his eye can be thus guided.

One of the Lord's eternal "shalls" comes in connection with guidance: "Trust in the Lord with all thine heart, and lean not unto thine own understanding. In all thy ways acknowledge him, and he shall direct they paths" (Prov. 3:5-6).

Guidance in Prayer

The Holy Spirit not only guides to whom to speak, he guides for whom to pray.

When in China, it was my custom to pray for

Chinese in the morning, as I felt that they most needed the Lord when awake and targets for the devil. At my evening prayer time, I prayed for my family and American friends who were beginning their days and would face temptation or opportunity.

One evening, when presenting my family one by one to the Lord, I came to Broadus, my youngest brother. There was nothing that I could ask the Lord to do for him. I said, "Lord, Broadus is alright, I leave him with you."

The next morning I received a cable announcing that Broadus had passed on from pneumonia the afternoon before. The Lord would not let me pray for the dead.

All Spirit-filled people experience times when the Holy Spirit lays on their hearts people for whom they are especially to intercede.

8

SINS FORGIVEN UP TO DATE

The Holy Spirit, through Paul, urged his son in the Lord, Timothy, to follow them that call upon the Lord out of a pure heart.

Just before the Japanese invasion of China reached our section of West Shantung, I did something which I had always refused to do. I took into our mission school all of the non-Christians who wanted to come. Since one non-Christian, especially in a boarding school, could create more atmosphere than ten Christians produced, it has been my custom to take in only a small number at a time so that we might always have a Christian atmosphere.

All Chinese government schools were closed before the Japanese Army reached our city, and teachers went West to keep ahead of the Japanese army.

As the Japanese took the cities, they opened schools, forcing any Chinese capable of teaching to do so. Japanese soldiers were assigned to teaching staffs to teach the Japanese language and to lead the daily ceremony of worshiping the emperor of Japan.

Needless to say, our mission school soon had all who possibly could crowd in. Young people from the finest old non-Christian families in the city came. I considered them to be our evangelistic opportunity.

We taught Bible in our school just as we did history, and we had a thirty-minute period of worship daily. All met at the school on Sunday morning and went to Sunday School and church. We did not force anyone to go to church. You see, we just had our school customs, and when students chose our school they accepted our customs.

Not being able to teach all of the Bible, I secured the finest Chinese Bible teacher in North China for that purpose, Miss Kiang Pao Shan. She was the grandchild of Christians, and as long as she could remember had been taught about the Lord, and to memorize

Bible passages. She went through mission schools from first grade through junior college, then took three years' work in seminary. She had gone through that great revival in North China, where she received a special anointing of the Lord for teaching the Word.

Not only did Miss Kiang spend hours in preparation of material to be taught, but before going to each class she got on her knees with the roll of that class before her and presented those students one by one to the Lord, asking him to take that material which would be considered that day to the heart of each pupil, whether Christian or non-Christian.

Our city, Tsining, on Grand Canal in Shantung Province, fell to the Japanese on January 11, 1937. We worked with the Chinese under a Japanese government for four years.

In the autumn of 1941, the State Department of our Government, seeing Japanese attitude getting worse toward the United States, sent a cable asking women and children to return to the United States. No missionary who is well in body ever is willing to leave the work and just return to the United States.

We single women said, "This does not mean "women and children" it means "women *with* children." We took the matter up with our Foreign Mission Board and were informed that the Board's desire was that all women with children should return to the United States, but that they were leaving single women to make their own decisions. Any who felt led of the Lord to return home should do so; others could remain on the field.

When the cable first was received, the Bible teacher, Miss Kiang Pao Shan, asked, "Miss Smith, what are you going to do about that cable which has come from your Government asking you to return to the United States?"

I answered, "I will go out into West China and keep on giving the gospel to the Chinese." I knew that I could not travel the roads where Japanese soldiers would be, but thought that I might go with a guide along the paths through the fields from village to village and eventually get across the Japanese lines and on out into West China, where I hoped the Japanese would never reach. However, I never felt led to start, so just remained where I was.

Some weeks afterward, when days were short, the sun setting at four P.M., when city gates were closed and locked and not opened until sunup the next morning, the Chinese head teacher of our mission school came out to my little house and asked me to call Miss Kiang from the girl's dormitory. He wanted the two of us to go out to his home nearby and pray for his sick baby. The only doctor was outside the city wall. Sunrise next morning might be too late for a sick baby.

We took our Chinese Bibles and went out to the little home, and wanting some word from the Lord on which to base our petition, I turned to 1 John 3:22 and read, "Whatsoever we ask, we receive of him, because we keep his commandments, and do those things that are pleasing in his sight."

To my amazement, Miss Kiang said, "Teacher Ming" (my Chinese name), "I cannot pray for this sick baby!"

When I asked her trouble, she said, "There is a woman in our church whom I do not love. She offended me publicly more than a year ago, and from that day until this, I have had nothing to say to her. I only say good morning and pass on."

Miss Kiang knew the Lord well enough and his Word well enough to know that she could not come into the presence of Holy God and have him perform a miracle and heal a sick child if there were anything in her heart that grieved him.

We did not pray for that baby. We prayed for that sick Christian. We read passages from God's Word on forgiving people who sin against us, not just seventy times seven, but just as often as they sin against us, so often do we forgive them. When a Christian forgives a person, his attitude toward that person is as if that incident never had occurred.

Miss Kiang was better prepared for Christian work and more experienced than any woman in the local church. She had stood in the women's meeting and suggested some Christian work which the women might do. Miss Kiang had come from one of the oldest mission centers in Shantung Province, where the women could do much more practical mission work than the women of our new field. Mrs. Connely, in our American way of speaking straightforwardly, responded to Miss Kiang's proposition by saying, "That will not work in this section of undeveloped women." In the Chinese custom, Miss Kiang had been rebuked publicly. One's suggestion must always be accepted in public or the speaker will "lose face."

Miss Kiang's human pride had been offended and she could not take it! For a whole year she had harbored what she thought was an injustice. From God's Word, as it was read to her, she saw that it was her human pride which had been grieved when her suggestion was not accepted. It had taken an hour for her to see this, but when she did she began to weep before the Lord, and begged him to forgive her for having held that sin of unforgiveness in her heart for a whole year. She put that sin on Christ and thanked him for taking it in his own body to the cross. She not only thanked the Lord for his forgiveness, but told him that she would see Mrs. Connely before she went to school the next day, and beg her forgiveness.

I then read my Bible verse again, in preparation for praying for the sick baby: "Whatsoever we ask, we receive of him, because we keep his commandments, and do those things that are pleasing in his sight." Again I was astonished by Miss Kiang saying, "Teacher Ming, I cannot pray for this sick baby!"

When I asked what her other trouble was, she replied, "Do you recall that day that I asked what you were going to do about that message from your government asking you to return to the United States? You answered that you would go out to West China and just keep on giving the gospel to the Chinese. That statement has been a sword in my heart from this day until this. I am living that the Chinese people may know my Savior, but I am living in Shantung Province where my family and friends are. I have never given myself to the Lord to go away out somewhere and live among strangers that they might know my Savior!"

We did not pray for that sick baby! That woman knew the Lord well enough and she knew the Word of God well enough to know that she could not come into his holy presence and call upon him to perform a miracle and heal a sick baby unless she had placed herself unreservedly at his disposal. Since the day that she was saved, it had never been any business of hers where her human body was. All that she had to do was to find out where her "Commanding Officer" wanted her and put herself there. It would be no concern of hers what might happen to her.

We did not pray for that baby, but for that wonderful Christian worker with an unusual prayer life. We read passage after passage of what it cost God to save us, what it cost him for us to be able to escape the power of sin in this life and its consequences in the next.

Away in the night, that convicted woman pled with the Lord to forgive her for not having placed herself unreservedly at his disposal. She told the Lord that he could now send her anywhere on the face of the earth that he might want her to go to tell people about him. Then she added, "This is on one condition, I must know that you are sending me. If I know that, I will go no matter what may happen to me!"

That woman had gotten on praying ground. We united our hearts before the Lord and humbly asked him for his own glory to touch the body of that baby and heal it. We then went home and went to bed.

The next morning the baby was alright, and so was Miss Kiang. I am sure that she went by to see Mrs. Connely and got right with her, even though she had to be at class at eight o'clock. When she went to the first class, the students remarked, "Miss Kiang, you look so happy today." She acknowledged that she had had two sins in her heart which had grieved the Holy Spirit and kept her from bearing his fruit of love and joy in her heart.

As she went to other classes, she had the same experience. She met teachers in the hallway who asked, "Miss Kiang, why so radiant today?" She gave them testimonies, and by the end of the school day all knew that Miss Kiang was like a new person.

Classes closed at 4:45. At five o'clock, here came Mr. Wang, the father of the sick child who had been healed (and six Christian boys) to my little home. He said, "Call Miss Kiang over from the girl's dormitory. We want you and her to pray for us that we may have the joy in our hearts that she has today."

We prayed with them until supper time. After supper, two men teachers and ten Christian boys came, making the same request, and adding, "We want the joy which Miss Kiang and Mr. Wang and those boys who were over here this afternoon have."

Miss Kiang and I took them one by one and brought them to the foot of the cross, to transfer every sin in their hearts and lives to the One who took them to the cross. It was ten o'clock that night when they were ready to return to their dormitory rejoicing.

The next afternoon, there was another roomful, and after supper the same. When all of the Christian boys and men teachers had gotten on praying terms with the Lord, and were bearing the fruit of the Spirit, the Christian girls and women teachers began coming. Now what do you suppose happened when they all got right with the Lord?

Those unsaved students who had been hearing the Word and studying it now saw a living Lord in the hearts and lives of their teachers and fellow students, and they wanted him! A few had been saved during that four years, some even having led their parents to the Lord, but most of them had not dared to take a stand against their Buddhist grandparents and infidel parents.

Every afternoon until supper time, 6:30, and until ten in the evening, my little study and living room were full of students on their knees getting right with Holy God. For a whole month I did not have ten minutes to walk for exercise after school hours. I did not miss it or even think of it.

Then last, a small group still unsaved expected to come on the afternoon of December 7, 1941, but that morning when I went to school, Japanese soldiers stepped up to the school entrance and asked me to take the teachers around the corner to our residence yard, saying that they would be responsible for the school.

I had been the one to face the Japanese alone for nine months after they took our city, so after the Connelys returned, I always went for him when the Japanese appeared. When I reached our residence yard, there he stood with a half-dozen Japanese soldiers around him. He said, "Go back and call your teachers. They have come to shut us up. They say that the United States and Japan are at war."

For the next six months, no one came to my house, nor did I go out, until I walked out the gate to come to the United States on the first Gripsholm, a Swedish steamer bringing United States citizens in exchange for Japanese who were in the United States.

However, the few unsaved students did not need me to lead them to the Savior. Their own teachers and fellow students could do that. Not only were they saved, but a real reviving began in the church. Mr. Wang, the head teacher, was superintendent of the Sunday School and song leader, as well as a deacon. Teachers who had become flames taught grown people. Young people with

testimonies taught Intermediates. And Intermediates
who had gotten their sins forgiven up-to-date taught
Juniors.

How did that getting right with God start? With one
key woman who not only was willing to confess her sins
and lay them on Christ, but who humbled herself and
confessed to the one wronged, according to our Lord's
instructions in Matthew 5:23-24: "If thou bring thy
gift to the altar, and there rememberest that thy brother
hath aught against thee; leave there thy gift before the
altar, and go thy way; first be reconciled to thy brother,
and then come and offer thy gift."

Miss Kiang was cleansed, first, by confessing God and
transferring the sin to the cross; then she made apology
to the one against whom she had sinned. She could
then dedicate her cleansed personality to the Lord. She
had thought before that she was dedicated, but she
could not dedicate sin. So long as she had not handed
her cleansed personality over to the Lord for his complete possession, she was living a rebel, with self enthroned. This so grieved the Holy Spirit that he could
not produce his fruit in her.

9

MOSES' PRAYER

"Therefore he said that he would destroy them, had not Moses his chosen stood before him in the breach, to turn away his wrath, lest he should destroy them" (Ps. 106:23).

Often at the beginning of a prayer retreat I use for Bible study the prayer of Moses.

Less than forty days after Israel at Sinai had trembled over the mighty voice of God pealing forth his standard of holiness for Israel, the people begged Aaron to make false gods for them. From their golden earbobs, rings, and bracelets, Aaron made a golden calf.

Moses was on the mountain receiving instructions from God. He had been fasting there for forty days when Holy God looked down and saw the idol worship. God determined to blot out the nation and make a new start with Moses' family. What an opportunity for Moses, who had given up the glories of Egypt and followed sheep in the desert for forty years for Israel.

It had been only forty days since Israel had heard God's rolling voice peal forth from the reeling, burning Sinai, "I am the Lord thy God, which brought thee out of the land of Egypt. . . . Thou shalt not make unto thee graven images. . . . Thou shalt not bow down thyself to them, nor serve them" (Ex. 20:1-5) .

Not only had the calf been made, but sacrifices had been offered to it. The Israelites, who were daily eating God's bread from heaven, gave God's glory to that calf. Thirty thousand of them removed their clothes and danced around the calf, stealing God's glory and giving it to a dumb idol.

When Jehovah God looked down and saw such idolatry, he knew that they deserved death. He refused to be identified with Israel any longer.

While they were down in Egypt he constantly referred to them as "my people." To Moses, he said, "Go tell Pharoah to let my people go!" When he saw them worshiping that idol, he refused to call them his people. (To Moses, he said, "Go, get thee down; for thy people, which thou broughtest out of the land of Egypt, have corrupted themselves" (Ex. 32:7) .

Moses knew they were not his people. He never could have gotten them out of Egyptian bondage. How could he have sent the plagues to Egypt, saved the lives of oldest sons, or opened the Red Sea at the right time to save Israel and close it to destroy the Egyptian army? He cast the people back on the Lord, "Why doth thy wrath wax hot against thy people, which thou hast brought forth out of the land of Egypt with great power, and with a mighty hand?" (v. 11) .

The Lord asked Moses not to pray for the people below who had corrupted themselves, just let him alone to destroy them. He would carry out his purpose to make Israel a great nation by sending the Savior through the descendents of Moses. Moses acted as if he had not even heard God's proposition; he prayed anyway. He boldly pled for God to turn away his fierce wrath.

He faced the mighty God with his own reputation. God's honor and glory were at stake. The Egyptians would hear about it and get the wrong impression of God. They knew him as a God of great power and wrath. If Israel should be destroyed, the Egyptians would think that he in his wrath and power destroyed them just because they did not do to please him. Egyptians would not know that God was a God of loving mercy who forgives. God, for his own honor and reputation, must not destroy Israel (see Ex. 32).

Next, he pled God's own word to Abraham, Isaac, and Jacob, to whom he had promised to take Israel back to the land. To Jacob, Jehovah God had foretold the location in the land, of the twelve tribes, and that the Savior would come through Judah (Gen. 49:10). God could not destroy Israel and be true to his promise. Moses was of the tribe of Levi. When Moses pled God's honor and his own word, Jehovah God changed his mind about destroying Israel; but he had the leaders put to death. Moses thus, by his praying, had saved the physical lives of the people of the nation. He had stood in the gap and turned away God's holy wrath.

Moses went down and had thirty thousand of the calf worshipers put to death.

Holy God said to Moses, "Say unto the children of Israel, Ye are a stiffnecked people: I will come up into the midst of thee in a moment and consume thee."

The children of Israel removed their ornaments and mourned and wept in repentance. Moses did not excuse the people for their sins. He rebuked them by saying, "Ye have sinned a great sin, and now I will go up unto the Lord; peradventure [it may be] I shall make an atonement for your sin."

Moses returned to the Lord to seek his forgiveness. "I [Moses] fell down before the Lord, as at the first, forty days and forty nights: I did neither eat bread, nor drink water, because of all your sins, . . . in doing wickedly in the sight of the Lord, to provoke him to anger. For I was afraid of his anger and hot displeasure, wherewith the Lord was wroth against you to destroy you" (see Deut. 9:17-20).

Moses did not excuse the people before Jehovah God, but said, "This people have sinned a great sin, and have made themselves gods of gold."

Here Moses won the title "The Meekest Man." What does meek mean? Not "weakness!" Meekness means *selflessness*. Certainly Moses deserved the title.

Next, Holy God assured Moses that Israel could go on into Canaan, but that he himself would not go with them, lest in his anger toward their sin he might consume them. Even though he would not go, he would permit them to go and he would send an angel to accompany them.

Perhaps you and I would have said, "By sin we have lost God's presence. We do no longer deserve to have him with us. We will have to get along the best we can with the angel." But not Moses! He knew the crowd with whom he was dealing. An angel would not do for Moses in that situation.

This shocked the people into more repentance.

Moses continued to plead the very presence of the mighty God with them. "Unless thou go with us, take us not up hence!"

After punishing Israel with plagues, the Lord assured

Moses that he would go with them and give him rest.

Moses' intercession accomplished several things:

First, because he did not let God alone, Holy God granted his request and saved their physical lives.

Second, because merciful God loves to forgive and he had a Moses to cooperate with him in pleading with him to do what had been his first will to do, God could forgive the terrific sin.

Third, he gained for Israel that Jehovah God might dwell in their midst, lead them into the land, drive out the seven warring nations there, give peace, and dwell among them.

Fourth, he received for himself that which he had not asked! The glory of the Lord reflected in his own countenance!

That kind of prayer cost Moses:

First, it cost his family. Moses died to himself and to his family. Moses could have been the head of a great race like Abraham.

Second, the Savior could have come through his descendants.

Third, it cost the forty days and nights of physical and heart agony as he stood in the gap.

What do you accomplish by your praying? I will answer this for you by another question. How much does your praying cost you? God needs people to stand in the gap. God needs people to cooperate with him to accomplish his will for others.

PART FOUR

GOING ON

10

BEWARE OF SPECIAL EXPERIENCES CALLING ATTENTION TO SELF

Speaking in Tongues

I have been amazed to find so much of this among Baptists in the United States. A few years ago I spent a week with the Woman's Missionary Union in Houston. By combining the churches in various sections of the city, I was able to reach more than two hundred churches in the week.

After returning to my room from a day's session, the telephone would ring and a woman's voice would say something like this: "I detect from your message that you have been filled with the Holy Spirit." I replied in the affirmative. Then the woman asked if I had spoken in tongues. I answered no, and she began to try to convince me that I was missing the biggest part of being a Christian.

At one of the larger churches of Fort Worth, a lawyer came to the services and sat in the middle row near enough for me to discern the expression on his face as I gave the message. He looked as if to say, "What on earth is that woman talking about?" One evening he asked the pastor if he could take me back to the motel.

All the way there and sitting in the car in front of the door to my room for two hours, that man tried to persuade me that I should speak in tongues.

The only reason I got from him was that it had revived a useless man who had been baptized into a country church when he was a boy, meaning nothing to the church, or to the Lord, or to anyone.

A woman went to his law office early in his career and told him that what he needed was to speak in tongues. He said that he does it now for "personal edification." He surely did not appear edified! What does "edify" mean? To build up. Certainly feeding his soul on the Word and communing with his Father in prayer edifies. Sharing the Lord and his riches with others edifies. Making money to give to the Lord's work edifies. I cannot understand how producing some sounds with the vocal organs which one does not understand can build up the spiritual life.

Of the people whom I have known personally who spoke in tongues, only a very few have gone on higher with the Lord. Some have gone off on tangents in beliefs or Christian practices, and others have become depressed or upset nervously.

One thing about it which I do not understand is that no one filled with the Holy Spirit of whom I have heard has ever spoken in tongues unless associated with someone else who did so. Now, if this is from the Lord, why do people not speak with tongues when filled with the Holy Spirit, even though they have not been blessed through some preacher who did, or were influenced by someone who had?

I am asked often if the people whom I lead to be filled with the Holy Spirit speak in tongues at my

Christian Life Conferences or prayer retreats. My reply is, "No, because they do not know about it."

If it is from the Lord, what could it matter whether or not the speaker of the time did or did not?

Twice I heard something in prayer which may have been called praying in tongues. It was not in a meeting, just in prayer with two or three.

A devout Chinese woman and I were praying together over a serious situation in the church where we worked in North China. We were sorely burdened and crying for the Lord to undertake in the matter. Suddenly the woman went off into utterances which I did not understand, but my heart kept crying to the Lord in perfect harmony with hers. I never let her know but that I thought she was speaking perfect Mandarin. I feared the devil would make her proud of having done something special. The next Sunday morning the man causing the trouble arose and humbly confessed his wrong to the church. I still kept the woman's prayer secret. I thought that the Lord wanted only the two of us to know about it.

The second instance was when a Chinese Christian worker and I were praying with a Chinese Bible teacher whom we recognized as a Spirit-filled woman. As we humbled ourselves under the mighty hand of God, he opened the windows of heaven and filled our souls with joy unspeakable.

All that I could do was kneel at my chair and laugh, knowing that I could not control my vocal organs to put into words my praise. I did not try. The Bible teacher, in her effort to express her praise, went into sounds which I did not understand, but my heart was one with her praising the Lord.

It seems wise to share in public those blessings that are given publicly and to keep secret those received in private. If some are given ability to speak in an "unknown tongue" in private, as Paul enjoyed, would it not be safer to keep them in private?

Could the first case have been the Holy Spirit praying through the woman with groanings which could not be expressed in human language (Rom. 8:26) ? If he prays with groans, could he not also praise with unexpressible ecstasy?

Or, could it have been in both experiences that the women were trying to talk to the Lord when they could not control their vocal organs to do so?

I am convinced from the testimony of many that sometimes the devil enables people to speak in tongues to deceive them and get their eyes on gifts and experiences instead of keeping their eyes on the Lord.

I have a good friend, who is now in glory, who resigned from teaching Bible in a Christian college to give all of his time to teaching the Word to pastors and church leaders. He built a chapel on his lot and opened Bible classes in the autumn, and for nine months he taught three classes daily. People drove as much as sixty miles once a week to the class. He reached many preachers.

One of his vacation projects was a Bible conference at Glade Valley where he rented a mountain academy building. I was one of his speakers for a number of years.

Quite gleefully, he told me one summer, "Miss Bertha, I have heard a man speak in tongues." He then told me of three men praying together one evening, when one said to the other two, "The Lord has given me the interpretation." My friend told me of the interpretation—the truth of which can be found in many places in the New Testament.

I thought, "Now, this is strange; the Lord knows English, and each of those men speak English, and since the Lord never misuses his power, why would he go in a roundabout way to give those two men a message? Why did he not give them the chapter and verse of some book in the Bible?"

The Bible teacher went on to tell me the effect of the message in the "unknown tongue." He said that he had never had such an emotional uplift. He lay awake for hours that night as if in the third heaven, so elated was he.

When he had finished describing the experience, I asked, "Do you suppose that could have come from the devil?" He just looked at me, and I said no more.

The next summer when I went to the conference and saw my friend, he said, "Miss Bertha, when you suggested that the glorious experience which I had when hearing a man speak in tongues might have come from the devil, you just bolted me over! It had never occurred to me that it was from any other than the Lord. I am now convinced that the whole thing was from the devil."

He learned later that the one who had given the "message" was so full of sin the Lord could not have worked a miracle through him.

The devil knew the influence of the Bible teacher and wanted to get him off on a tangent to hurt his ministry.

I had not realized until that time that the devil also counterfeits joy. I had known before of his counterfeiting all other gifts. But I learned that we had better be informed on the wiles of the devil as well as looking out for his onslaughts.

I find many who are calling tongues a gift and connecting it with the Pentecost ability to speak in other languages. Yet, none of these in America have ever, so far as anyone knows, spoken in a language. Even though some have claimed to do so, those who knew that language found that it was not what the speaker thought.

Regarding Pentecost, many Gentiles over the Roman Empire had become worshipers of the true God. They joined with Jews from many countries, some of whom had been born abroad, in Jerusalem for the observance of the spring festivals.

At Pentecost, many nationalities heard the Word preached in their own languages. The apostles spoke languages to the people present at Pentecost, according to the Word, "as the Spirit gave them utterance."

The next case was Cornelius, the Roman official stationed at Caesarea who had given up his heathen religions and was, to the best of his knowledge, worshiping the God of the Jews. He did not know that the Savior had come. God saw the eagerness of his soul to worship the true God, and sent an angel down to tell him where to find a man who could make such worship possible. Only a saved man could do that, so the angel directed Cornelius to Peter. Cornelius sent three soldiers down that fifty-mile sandy road along the Mediterranean to tell Peter to come. Peter had never eaten with a Gentile up to that time, and would not have gone had the Lord not prepared him by a vision when he was praying on his host's housetop. Peter, even after the vision, would not go without taking six saved Jews with him (Acts 11:12).

It is recorded that as soon as Peter and his party arrived and began to speak that the Holy Spirit fell upon them and they spoke with tongues. Peter and the six saved Jews whom he took with him accepted this as evidence that the Gentile group had been saved and filled with the Holy Spirit. They later reported by saying, "The Holy Spirit fell on them just as he did on us at the beginning" (see Acts 11:15). God gave them the like gift as he did unto us who believed on the Lord Jesus Christ: Had they not spoken languages, it would not have been just as it was at Pentecost.

The purpose for which Cornelius and his household spoke with tongues was a miracle granted by the Lord to show to the Jerusalem Church that God was the God of every race and that Jesus Christ was the Savior of all nations.

The next time men spoke with tongues was for the same reason. The twelve men at Ephesus whom Paul found were not saved. Someone who had heard John the Baptist's message had preached it to them, and they accepted it as far as it went. How do we know that they had not been saved? Because Paul had them baptized; they no doubt were Gentiles. Had they been Jews, they would have known from the Old Testament about the Holy Spirit.

When they were filled, they spoke with tongues for the same purpose that the miracle was granted to Cornelius, which was that the Jewish Christians in Jerusalem were forcing all Gentiles to become Jews by ceremony before they could be saved.

Thus, the argument which Peter and Paul used in the conferences with the Jerusalem Church, recorded in Acts 11 and 15, won freedom for the Gentiles to be saved by faith.

The "tongues" question in Acts is no problem. We can see why the Holy Spirit spoke through the believers as he did. The only problem in the Bible concerning this question is in that backslidden church in Corinth. They were so backslidden that the tongues question was not their only problem. Paul called them "carnal, babes" to whom he could only feed the milk of the Word. He had to get along with them the best he could. Even so, he threatened to go to them with a stick and give them a beating for allowing gross sin in the church.

The experience with the tongues in the Corinthian church had nothing to do with the kind of miracle which the Holy Spirit wrought at Pentecost. Note that at Pentecost it was the Holy Spirit who gave the apostles utterance when they spoke languages. At each of the other instances in the Acts, it was when the Holy Spirit filled them that they spoke in other languages. The Corinthians certainly were not filled with the Holy Spirit. If they ever had been they were not when Paul's letters were written to them. As was stated above, no one there spoke languages. It is not stated anywhere that the Holy Spirit spoke through them; Paul would have given no regulations for controlling the speaking of the Holy Spirit in the meetings. It was "their speaking" which Paul regulates. No one today knows just what that was or why they did it. It could have been that when it started that they spoke the languages of the different nationalities present, and God gave others the ability to interpret so that all could know what was being said, and later they became proud of it, and others wanted to do the same. Corinth was a cosmopolitan city, probably with several nationalities. There could have been some in the Corinthian church who did not speak Greek.

When Dr. Charles Leonard went from North China to North Manchuria to open mission work, he was the only Protestant missionary in the great city of Harbin. His church services were translated into Japanese for the Christians among those invaders. There were many white Russians there who had fled from Russia when Communists took that country, so someone translated the message into Russian. His being the only church service for British and American business people who were there, the message was put into English.

Four nationalities heard the messages, and each just sat and waited for each sentence to pass through four mouths, and were glad to hear the Word preached even at that. Brother Leonard would have preached an hour; his services lasted the whole forenoon, after getting an early start!

Corinth could have had a similar situation in their church. Those who had the gift of languages could have become the envy of the others. Certainly Paul spoke something which was not a human language, but he had been caught up to third heaven, and may have gotten the language up there.

Anyway, let us remember that he said to the Corinthians, "In the church I had rather speak five words with my understanding . . . than ten thousand words in an *unknown* tongue" (1 Cor. 14:19). The word "unknown" is written in italics in the King James Version, which means that the word is not in the original language. It has been so put by the interpreters, so they think, to clarify the meaning.

First Corinthians 14:33: "God is not the author of confusion, but of peace, as in all churches of the saints." When I am asked if I speak in tongues, my reply is, "Had the Lord given me the Chinese language, I would have been much obliged, but I had to dig it out for myself. One does not pick it up. I do not praise him half enough in the two languages which I speak. Furthermore, I take the Lord for my example, not Paul. I would have to be caught up into the third heaven before I could follow Paul. I am supposed to express the Lord Jesus Christ through *my* personality, not Paul's. My Lord never spoke anything that others did not understand when he was on earth, as recorded in the Word.

It is a known fact that the devil takes advantage of this sometimes and uses it for himself just to get the Lord's children confused. When he sees that a person is going all the way with the Lord and he cannot stop him, his next strategy is to thrust him out in front of the Lord, to do things that later will get his mind on himself instead of upon the Lord. Many have acknowledged later that the devil made them speak in tongues.

My tongue is the Lord's. He can take hold of it anytime that it will please him and produce any kind of sounds that he wants to for his own glory, but I surely do not want to give place to the devil, to excel, or try to prove that I am spiritual. Even some denominations which try to take the Corinthian church experience back into Pentecost and connect it with the fullness of the Holy Spirit actually teach people how to speak in tongues.

We praise the Lord for any individual or group that

is getting people saved and filled with the Holy Spirit, and some of these people are doing that, but we cannot accept what they teach that is wrong just because they are being used to teach some of the Word that is right. The Lord uses his Word that is preached to get people saved and to lead them to let the Holy Spirit fill them, but that does not mean that we can accept other teachings which are not according to the Word.

A friend left the Baptist faith because she was heart-hungry, and she saw a sick woman healed at a Pentecostal meeting. "That was it," she thought. She had a new experience with the Holy Spirit. They teach that the sinful nature is eradicated so that they will not sin any more. At first she thought that her sin was eradicated. After awhile she began to have an "accident" occasionally, and as time went on she saw that the other church members were no more eradicated than she. She humbly returned to a Baptist church. She still has a deep appreciation for Pentecostals so far as they are right, but she sees that some of their teachings are so wrong that she could not say to the world, by being a member of their church, "This is what I believe that the Bible teaches."

Pride in Service

One of the devil's chief strategies for Christian workers is to make them proud of their service. Christian lay people are apt allies of the devil as they brag on those who are in positions of leadership. At the associational and convention meetings, speakers and those who make reports are lauded for their good jobs until the Holy Spirit must be too quenched to remain in the assembly.

If the Lord has been able to use the person, all the

glory should go to him.

It is unsafe to let others know how much time you spend in prayer or how early you arise for the same.

One of my wise seminary teachers admonished students, "Pray all night just as often as you like, but be sure that you never let anyone know about it!"

The same is true of fasting, of prayer, or of special giving to the Lord's work.

Jesus knew sinful nature when he urged his hearers not to let the left hand know what the right did.

We sometimes see valuable servants of the Lord get such an exalted opinion of themselves that the Lord must prune them by bringing them down to smaller opportunities, or not use them at all.

It is easy to be unconscious of the pride which other people see.

It may be because of appearances, natural ability, education, or even family heredity, which is so appreciated and relied upon that the Holy Spirit is too grieved to do his work.

11

RESIST THE DEVIL

The devil is not just an influence, but a supernatural personality of great power, whom we are admonished to resist *steadfast in the faith* (1 Pet. 3:9). Because he is the archenemy of our Lord and Savior Jesus Christ, whom he aspired too supercede in the glory, and because he cannot now attack Christ, he attacks us (Luke 10:18; Isa. 14:12-18).

When working in our mission boys' school in Chefoo, an American Young Woman's Christian Association secretary with whom I had been in Peking language school called on me. When I spoke of the trouble the devil caused in the school, she said, "Bertha, you know that you do not believe in a personal devil!" I thought, *My friend, you start snatching people out of his clutches and you will discover something of the powerful personality that he is. However, so long as you are satisfied to continue planting trees and seeing where women spit in hairnet factories, you never will know that he is a ferocious being with indescribable power, and living in Chefoo!*

Praise the Lord. The devil is not all powerful. "Greater is he that is in you, than he that is in the world" (1 John 4:4). The Lord in us wants to be conqueror over the devil and all of his demons. He will be if we cooperate with him. We do not have the power, but the Lord has given to us the authority to call down the Lord's power over the enemy.

How May We Be Conquerors?

First, we must give no place to the devil (Eph. 4:27). Any unconfessed, unforsaken sin, or doubtful habit is a place for the devil to take hold. We must keep clean and holy all the time. What does it mean to be holy? We must not only keep all sin cleansed, but the old unholy self must be dethroned, or kept in the place of death, with Christ enthroned in his stead by a definite act of the will.

Next, we store our minds with promises of God and quote them in the face of every temptation, and continually repeat them audibly.

We Conquer by Prayer

This, too should be spoken audibly. We pray to God against the devil, to take authority over the devil and all of his demons. Command him in words loud enough for him too hear, and emphatically, to get out of the situation and stay out!

Do not refer to him and his strength and wiles too much. Keep your eyes on the Lord and his might, and keep praising him, with no mention of the devil, unless his presence is recognized. My mother taught her children not to make too much of the devil. She said that he *likes* "honorable mention." Do not magnify him. Be sure continually to magnify the Lord, but do not fail to deal with him if his presence is felt.

We Conquer by Fasting

God's standard set for Israel at Sinai was that all males must go to the tabernacle or Temple three times a year for worship: during the Passover and Pentecost in the spring and the great day of Atonement in autumn.

Preceding the worship was a time when they fasted and afflicted their souls in repentance of sin and made the sin offering. This was followed by the peace and other offerings. Women and children went along with the men because it was a gala time, seeing all of their friends and feasting on the meat of the peace offerings.

Later in Israel's history we see people fasting in prayer when in distress. David fasted and prayed for a sick child to be spared. The psalmist called upon Israel to fast as if it were work. David humbled himself and put on sackcloth and prayed for the subjects that were sick (Ps. 35:13). The psalmist speaks of his knees being weak from fasting (109:24). In Isaiah's time, Israel was so backslidden and full of sin in the heart that even though they kept up fasting it was not acceptable to the Lord (Isa. 58:5).

The Holy Spirit, through the prophet Joel, called upon the elders, citizens, and priests to observe a fast— to gird themselves, sit all night in sackcloth, and cry to the Lord in repentance. This was making work of fasting and praying. (Orientals belted down their lose garments which would hinder their work.)

A classic example of fasting is that of Daniel. In Babylon, Daniel had a copy of the prophecy of Jeremiah, from which he learned that it was God's purpose to keep Israel in captivity for seventy years, after which he would permit them to return to Jerusalem.

Knowing that the time was up, Daniel "set his face" to cooperate with the Lord and pray for his purpose to be fulfilled, by prayer and supplication, with fasting and sackcloth and ashes (Dan. 9).

In the deepest confession of the sins of their kings, princes, fathers, citizens, and including himself, he wept before the Lord, pleading for God's face again to shine on his people for God's own sake. God in his heaven heard and saw Daniel and sent Gabriel down to reveal to him the future of Israel. Jehovah God immediately moved the heart of the new heathen Persian king, Cyrus, not only to permit Israel to return to Jerusalem, but to be exceedingly abundant in providing for the same.

Zechariah rebuked Israel for fasting with the wrong purpose in view. Even during the seventy years Israel was kept in captivity in Babylon, they observed the spring and autumn fasts, but it was not accompanied by repentance and was not acceptable to the Lord (Zech. 7:6).

In our Lord's time, fasting had become an empty form in order to appear pious. The three fast days a year had been so multiplied that the Pharisees observed two fast days each week. They were not accompanied by repentance, sackcloth, ashes, or wailing over their sins. Neither Jesus nor his disciples observed these days.

Jesus began his ministry after having been anointed with the Holy Spirit and going away into the wilderness to fast forty days unto God.

He did not say much in his teaching about it because there was too much emphasis already in empty ritual. However, he gave his disciples a strong rebuke for not fasting on the following occasion.

We learn from Luke that Jesus was taking his disciples, the twelve, up to a mountain outside of the Jewish territory to get away from the committee of detectives sent by the Jewish Sandhedrin to follow him everywhere in an effort to find some charge for having him put to death.

It was the purpose of Jesus to take the disciples away up to a mountain to pray (Luke 9:28), to get them ready for his coming death. He had been sorely rebuked by Peter, who was speaking for the devil, telling him that he would not be killed in Jerusalem, when Jesus had just told the group that he would be and by Temple leaders. Jesus wanted them to get better prepared for what they would face in Jerusalem.

Peter, James, and John went on with Jesus up the mountain, and what a reward they received! Jesus took back some of his glory which he had in heaven, so that they could, without doubt, know that he was their Messiah, even though he would be put to death.

Moses came down. The Jews accused Jesus of having broken Moses's laws. He had not broken any of God's laws given through Moses, but he had broken the Jewish regulations right and left. Moses came down to let Jesus and the disciples present know that God approved of the way that Jesus had kept his laws.

Elijah, representing the prophets, came down to let the three know that Jesus was that Promised Prophet to come.

For the second time, they heard God the Father speak from heaven, "This is my beloved Son; hear him!" (When He tells you that he is going to die, you listen!)

They heard Moses and Elijah talking with Jesus

about his coming departure in Jerusalem. With what spring in their step the three must have gone down that mountain!

A poor helpless father had brought his demon possessed son to the nine that stayed below, to cast out the demons. In Mark 6:12-13, they went out and preached that men should repent, and they cast out many devils, and anointed with oil many that were sick and healed them.

Did they each one try to cast the demon out of the poor afflicted boy? Did Thomas say, "Let me try, I cast out one stronger than that!" Or did Andrew say, "I am sure that I can cast him out." Did Bartholomew or Thaddaeus perhaps try in confidence; or did Judas even take his turn?

What a situation these nine caused! They not only could not help the distressed father and give release to the boy in bondage, they even gave Jesus a bad reputation.

The committee from Jerusalem who had followed Jesus that far were there with the multitude, all in confusion because the demon had not obeyed the command of the nine to leave the boy.

The father, after such an experience with them, even doubted that Jesus could cast the demon out, "If thou canst," he implored.

Jesus could, always could, and always can! Even though that demon did his best to kill the boy, Jesus was equal to the occasion and rebuked the unclean spirit and healed the victim.

Later, when Jesus was alone with the disciples, they asked, "Why could we not cast the demon out?" They should have known without asking. His reply was,

"This kind goeth out only by prayer and fasting."

For twenty years, I have been fasting one meal a day when speaking. I give up the most important meal, which is dinner. It is the only sacrifice that I can make for a service, as I both enjoy fellowship with people and eating good food. This gives me a chance to go straight from the presence of the Lord to speak for him.

From the time that I began serving on public programs, there were always two statements which I wanted to make to the Lord just before getting up to speak. First, "Lord, I did not put myself on this program. I was invited to speak here and accepted it as being your appointment." Second, "I have not used time for myself which I should have used in preparation. I have done the very best that I could with the time that I had, now you take over and do the rest!"

About twenty years ago I learned that I was not doing all that the Bible speaks of, while through the years I had sometimes fasted when I had a burden of prayer, or in praying with other missionaries over some problem in the work and we agreed to fast.

I then began giving up a meal a day when in meetings. Since then, there are three things which I want to say to the Lord before getting up to speak—added to the two above: "Lord, I have for this service done everything that the Bible speaks of, now you take over and do the rest!" And he does!

I would not give it up for anything. I do not realize that I have not eaten, unless occasionally when praying with people after service until midnight, I sometimes feel weak. If so, I take a glass of milk.

12

INSTANT OBEDIENCE

Welcoming the Lord's Pruning!

All sin must be confessed up-to-date!

No one ever reaches the state where he will not sin anymore. The devil still is around to come at us through sinful human natures which are always trying to rise up and express themselves, even though they should be kept in the place of death. Sins of Spirit-filled people are accidents, never purposely planned. Accidental sins must be transferred from one's heart to the Lord Jesus Christ at once, trust in his blood for cleansing, again enthrone Christ, and ask the grieved Holy Spirit again to take over and fill. Then the Christian should go as if nothing has happened, except he should be more careful to trust the Lord to keep from such accidents.

After being filled, we have to learn how to *walk* in the Spirit. The first step is to obey the Lord.

There are past sins against people which must be made right by confessing to them and to others who may know about that sin. When everything is made right, we are ready to walk in the Spirit. Welcome the Lord's pruning.

One of my seminary professors advised us to have a pruning friend. (She then added, "The Lord will do it if you live closely enough to him and always obey.) "

One of my privileges on the mission field was that of living with Miss Martha Franks. We pruned each other frankly. We prayed together, taking about an hour to name before the Lord in united petition all the people with whom each of us worked, and others whom the Holy Spirit had laid on our hearts.

One day when we were praying, I was convicted of some wrong. I confessed it as sin and cried to the Lord for deliverance from it. When we arose from our knees, Martha looked at me most seriously and said, "Bertha, I must be living far, far from the Lord! It has been a long, long time since the Holy Spirit has convicted me of any sin. Don't you know that if I were walking closely enough with him, he would be pointing out things in me that he wants to change to make me more like himself!"

I sometimes walk into furniture stores where they have large floor plate mirrors. When I first get a glance of myself in them, I think, "A very nice looking woman!" But the closer I get to the mirror, the more clearly I see myself. When I am right in front of it, the wrinkles and freckles are so prevalent that I want to run out of the building.

Thus we are by our walk with the Lord. Satisfied with self means that we live so far from the Lord that either we cannot see his standard, or we are unwilling to be like him.

A Nickel Debt, a Dollar Payment

When I was about sixteen, I went by train to visit

my aunt for a week. In returning home it was necessary to wait two hours between trains in my home county seat.

Girls wore white China silk blouses that summer. I already had one, but there in a window was white China silk on sale! I went and bought material for another blouse and walked back to the railway station, thrilled over my bargain, until I learned that I lacked five cents having enough money for my ticket to my hometown, Cowpens!

What could I do? The dear Lord had provided a way for his worldly-minded child, by so arranging that two neighbors were awaiting the same train. Either of them would have lent me a nickel. But before the depression of the early thirties, it was bad taste indeed to let anyone know of any shortage in finances. (During the depression when everyone who had anything lost it, and all were in the same boat, that became the main topic of conversation. And alas, in listening at the average conversation we learned how much many lost, when they never had accumulated anything to lose.)

The devil is always handy to help one out in a situation to his own advantage, so he put it into my mind to purchase a ticket to Clifton, which I knew would cost five cents less than to Cowpens.

When we reached Clifton, the train waited longer than usual. The conductor then came in and asked, "Are you not getting off here?" "No," I said, "I am going to Cowpens." He admonished, "Always look at your ticket to see that it is punched right. Your ticket was punched to Clifton and I have been holding up the train for you to get off." The sinner answered, "Yes, sir."

Needless to say, I did not arrive at home elated over my "summer vacation," nor did I enjoy having *two* white China silk blouses!

Of course, I begged the Lord to forgive me, but I did not know that I would be forgiven upon confession of that sin.

Fifteen years later I learned that one cannot be right with God and wrong with anyone in the world. I wrote a letter to the ticket office of Spartanburg, Southern Railway, confessed that sin, and enclosed a one dollar bill; then I knew that the sin at last was settled!

Bertha and Her Beans

I had an object lesson on the sensitiveness of the Holy Spirit not long after I came home to retire.

A young preacher, Curtis McCarley, and his wife and son lived two miles out of Cowpens. They had become good friends of my sister Jennie and me. Their friends from Texas, a pastor and his wife and ten-year-old son, came to visit the McCarleys for a week.

It happened that my sister was away from home while they were there, but I invited our good friends and their guests for dinner one day anyway.

I love to cook and do all kinds of housekeeping, but I had not been home long or had a chance for much practice. I was not accustomed to cooking with electricity.

I wanted to have a good time with the Lord getting ready for them, as well as while they were there, so I planned well what I was going to do. Of course, I wanted everything to taste good and the house to be pretty. To avoid being rushed, I postponed my quiet time with the Lord until afternoon.

It was summer with plenty of flowers on the place, so

I put a pretty vase of them everywhere needed, got out the sterling, the crystal, and pretty china, and laid it all out on a pretty Chinese embroidered linen tablecloth, looking just right. I spent a happy morning singing and rejoicing in the Lord as I anticipated fellowship with the guests, perfectly sure that everything was going to be ready at the right time.

Five minutes before twelve-thirty, the hour set for dinner, the doorbell rang. Lo, I was just emptying a can of green beans into the pot! I was embarrassed over not having the dinner ready, and will never know why I gave the excuse that I did, except the fact that I am just *I*, and always will be the same old sinner, descendant of Adam, and subject to accidental sins.

I said, "Dinner will be a little late; one unit of the cook stove is burned out." Quite true, but I had three more, an oven, and a hot plate which were enough for the hot dishes in the summertime.

I sent the local couple into the parlor to show my Chinese things to their friends, and before long they were invited to the table, and we all had a delightful time indeed. After lunch, we got on our knees in the family living room and had a time of prayer. I do not recall, but suppose that I took my turn leading in prayer. I could not imagine myself refusing to pray when I had an opportunity.

After they had gone, I quickly cleaned up the kitchen and went upstairs and sat down with my Bible for awhile, and then got on my knees for my time of intercessory prayer. Lo! It was not prayer—no Lord there! My praying was not going higher that the ceiling! In astonishment, I asked, "Lord, what has happened? Why can I not pray?" It did not take long to find out.

The dear Lord, in his holy faithfulness, reminded me, "You did not tell your guests the truth! That dinner was not late because one unit of the stove was burned out." What I had not told them was that already I had burned up two pots of fresh green beans before I put in the canned ones!

How condemned! How could I have misrepresented the truth—no, just lied?

I had enough experience with the Lord in praying, and trying to pray when I could not, to know exactly what to do. I went downstairs to the back yard, got into my car, and drove out of town to the home of the McCarleys.

The two women were in the modern kitchen at the front. When I asked for the preachers, they called them from the study, and I said to the four of them, with all the humility of my soul, "I did not tell the truth as to why the dinner was late today; it was late because I had already burned up two pots of fresh green beans before the third pot."

The four looked at me as if to say in amazement, "What a missionary!" Not a one said a word. I turned around and fast as I could get out of there, I went back home and up to my room, and again got on my knees and found the Lord's ear open to my prayer.

13

MORE SUGGESTIONS FOR WALKING IN THE SPIRIT

To go forward in the Spirit-filled life there are some absolute essentials.

First: Testimony must be given. Spiritual blessings are to be shared. Cease to tell and soon there will be nothing to tell.

Second: You must constantly remind yourself that you by nature are no better than when you were saved. We have this treasure in earthen vessels. Why? That our new miraculous lives will be of God, and we will get no glory for them.

While we are no better after than before we are saved, we have a new position in God's sight. We must form new habits in the light of that position: habits of systematic Bible study and prayer; habits of keeping all sin confessed up-to-date (Confess immediately! Confess as widely as the sin is known. This is necessary for the sake of future testimony.) ; the habit of taking seriously the "checks"—where there is a restraint, stop and find out from the Lord what it is and take necessary steps immediately to remove the cause.

Third: It helps in going on with the Lord daily to

consider our new relationship to God. The Bible illus-
trates in several different ways our relationship to the
Triune God. We will here refer to only three:
> Citizens (Eph. 2:19).
> Children of God (1, John 3:2).
> Bride "The Spirit and the bride say, Come" (Rev.
> 22:17).

Citizens of Heaven

Let us first consider the relationship of being citizens
of the kingdom of heaven. We are citizens of heaven
temporarily residing in this world.

For more than 40 years, I was citizen of the United
States residing in China. On my first voyage to China
in 1917, Mary Nell Lyne and I took advantage of the
Japanese Railway offer to exchange steamer tickets for
railway tickets through Japan from Yokohama to Kobe.

We were passing through that section of Japan. Not
being citizens of that country, we did not put on Japanese kimnos and wooden clogs for shoes. We did not
cover our faces in white paste or wear our hair in huge
rolls over the tops of our heads, neither did we speak
their language nor eat their raw fish!

We were citizens of the United States, just passing
through Japan. If we always remember that we are citizens of heaven, not belonging to this world, would that
not solve our problems as to manner of dress, recrea-
tion, use of money, use of time, and influence?

Children of God

Those who have been born into the family of God
are called God's children. We become children of God
the day that we are born into his family—born of his

spirit. He stoops to call himself our Father.

The second way that we become children in a family is by adoption. A helpless child with no parents and no home is received into a home and legally becomes a child. He has no right there. He does not deserve that home, but because of the love and goodness of that man and wife, that child is received as their own, with all the privileges of a born son or a daughter.

It takes both of these illustrations—a physical birth in a home and an adoption—to illustrate our relationship to the Lord in being called his children. We are not born saved. God in his love reached out and snatched us out of the hand of the Evil One and brought us into his family and then put his life into us. How holy we should live in appreciation of our positions as children of God and heirs of all of his grace!

Children are supposed to favor their parents. Parents are happy for their children to look like them.

When a child and as a young woman, I went back to my grandmother's occasionally and went to church. The dear women in the community who knew grandmother's ten daughters and three sons came to speak to me, saying, "You must be Fannie's girl." When I proudly assented, they would say, "I see the favor!" Through the years when I came home on furloughs, the neighbors who came in to greet me invariably said, to my great delight, "The older Bertha gets, the more she favors her mother." When I looked around at my beautiful mother to see how she was responding to the thought of her ugly daughter looking like her, I saw the biggest smile on her face.

In my early years in Formosa, hundreds of Chinese who had been well-to-do on the China mainland and had forsaken all to escape communism camped in a cemetery near my home. My secretary and I led a Sunday School with them once a week, although not on Sunday. When the children saw the secretary coming, they ran to meet him and called to others, "Jesus is coming!"

Do people think of Jesus when they see you? Are you holy enough to favor him?

Parents have a standard for their children.

Godly parents do not permit their children to act and look like those from worldly homes. The daily customs of the family form a standard. For instance, they teach children instant obedience. Children are never consulted whether or not they will go to church, nor do they make them go or consult them at the table what they would like to eat. The family custom is that all go to church and eat what is served and children live according to the standard, without a word.

I heard Mr. Charles Hartwell, one of our North China missionaries, describe his leaving home to come to the United States to attend college. Miss Anna, his older sister, who already had returned to China as a missionary after having been recently in America, knew something of the life that he would enter. For weeks before his leaving, she warned and admonished. His saintly mother did her share of exhorting. The father said not a word until he extended his hand to his son to say goodby. He then said, "Charlie, don't you forget that your name is Hartwell!" Mr. Charles said he forgot practically all that sister Anna urged and most of his mother's injunction, but when temptation came he remembered his father's word, that he was named Hartwell. He knew there was a standard for the sons of that family and he must live up to them.

Children are to grow up useful to their parents. God's purpose for his children is that they become useful to him, become his wealth.

My father was a merchant and planter. He never took a vacation during his first twenty-one years after marriage. When he went North to buy goods for his store, he traveled at night going and coming; he just could not leave the store with hired clerks a day longer than necessary.

My oldest brother, wanting to be a merchant, majored in business and joined Father in the store. After that, Father began taking a month's vacation every August. Because he could trust his business to his son, he went all the way from South Carolina to Hot Springs, Arkansas, for complete relaxation. I heard him say that he was adding years to his life by taking a vaction.

The second son wanted to be a planter, and he attended the State Agriculture College. Lester, even before he went to college, was in the habit of taking thirty or forty day laborers to the plantation and leading them all day long at steady work. He picked 600 pounds of cotton in one day. I overheard my father say to my mother, "Lester is worth a thousand dollars a year to me on the plantation." (A thousand dollars was money in 1905.) Those two sons were father's wealth. He could entrust his affairs to them, knowing that they would be faithful.

Just how faithful are we in our Father's affairs which have been entrusted to us? Are there people already in hell whom the Lord could not save by himself because we were unconscious of being God's wealth?

God is helpless in showing himself to others without

us. It is only in the saints that he can live. Our hearts are the only throne that he has down here in this world. Are there folk around us living for self whom the Lord wanted to prepare to proclaim his Gospel in many lands; but the Lord could not win them because he was so very poor in their parents, or in their Sunday School teachers, Church Training leaders, or even in their pastors? Are you as a Christian worker trying to make a name for *yourself*, or are you just being God's wealth?

Some children are of no value; some are even problems. A woman in my home community had a little son who seemed all right for the first few months of life; but, when it came time for him to crawl, he didn't, and later he could not stand or walk. Year by year his body grew, until he was about twelve years old, then he stopped growing.

The only word that he ever learned to say was a call for his mother, "Ma!" He could not live without her. She looked after him as if he were a babe in arms, for no one else would do.

She loved the Lord, but for twenty-two years was unable to attend church.

He had a mother upon whom he depended for everything. He cried and called if she were out of his sight. Did that mother have a son? No! She had no son in him, only a burden. Is this like many to whom the Lord is their hope? In such, he has no son to be of use to him.

What a contrast to those for whom Paul prayed in the church at Ephesus (Eph. 1:18): "That ye may know what is the hope of his calling, and what the riches of the glory of his inheritance in the saints."

Bride of Christ

There is no closer fellowship on earth than that of man and wife. God calls them one. In the Old Testament, Jehovah God called Israel his wife. We hear the wail of the prophets as they pled with backslidden Israel, speaking for God: "Return unto me, for I am married unto you!"

In the New Testatment we are called the Bride of Christ. I have never heard a message on this, but I did some thinking on it one day and reached some reasons for our being called the "Bride of Christ."

First, brides are chosen, and so are we. We read in Ephesians 1:4 that we were chosen in him before the foundation of the world. The man chooses for his bride the person with whom he wants to associate for the remainder of his life. The young woman loves the man who loves her. A girl will leave home and go to the ends of the earth with a man if she is convinced that he loves her.

We are loved with an everlasting love that can never through time or eternity cool.

A woman proves her love by giving up for the one who loves her. She gives up other friends, not only her boyfriends but most of her girlfriends. She gives up her home, her family, and even her name. She gives up her way of living and lives to please her husband. She gives up her home community and goes with him anywhere that he needs to go.

She and the bridegroom want to be alone together. Who ever saw a bride and groom take their friends when they go on their honeymoon! Is that why I am called the Lord's bride? Does he want me to himself? How much do I respond to that kind of love?

When my sister had been married a year, I went to visit her. She had married the fourth of five sons, four of whom were away while he stayed at home on the plantation with his widowed mother. Sister Pearle said to me while I was her guest, "John and I never have any time to be alone." They had a big home, a kitchen and dining room on one end of the house, a family living room, and back of that the old lady's room, and then a hallway and beyond that a parlor, which was seldom used. No one but sister and her beloved used the upstairs. They had three porches and plenty of yard and big trees. It seemed to me there were plenty of places for her and John Brown to hold hands and look at the moon!

What did she mean, saying that she and John never had any time to be alone? She was so dead in love with John Brown that she wanted to sit down at the table and eat with him three times a day, and she did not want anyone else there! She couldn't get enough of being alone with the one whom she loved.

Now, how much do you like to be alone with the Lord? Is that a test of your love?

Did you hear of the two United States soldiers in a German prison during World War II, in adjoining cells? One said to the other, "This is hell being shut up here alone!" The other replied, "This is heaven getting away from everybody in this war, shut up with my Lord and Savior!" The happy one told the other how he was saved. He handed his New Testament through the iron bars to him, called out passages for him to read, and together they discussed them. The miserable one saw his lost condition and what God had done about his sin in Christ. He got on his knees in that cell and came as a sinner to the cross, transferring all of his sins and his sinful self to the Savior. Then, since they were no longer on him, he could receive the living Lord into his heart. His little cell, too, became a little heaven on earth.

The first reason for a young man to choose a bride is for fellowship. The second reason is that he wants a family and must have a bride to have children. Is that the reason that I am put in the position of a bride? The Lord is not willing that any should perish, but that all should come to repentance (2 Pet. 3:9). Paul called those whom he had won to the Lord his sons in the Lord (1 Tim. 1:1; Titus 1:4).

Then, I am to be faithful to him in leading people to be brought into his family. How many children do you have in the Lord?

In speaking this message, I usually begin by showing a big doll dressed in beautiful bridal attire. Then, I show another bride doll with her beautiful bridal gown just covered with black spots. (The spots, of course, represent sin.) When the great revival was in its early years in North China, one of the women missionaries dreamed one night that the Lord came to her dressed in the most beautiful white robe that she had ever seen. As he came forward, her eyes were fastened on that dazzling robe. When he was near enough to speak, he said to her, "Look down at your own robe." When she did, she saw that what had been a white robe was just covered with black spots. He said, "When you were saved, I clothed you in a pure white robe. Why did you get it all spotted and dirtied up like that?" When that young woman awoke the next morning, she jumped out of bed, got on her knees, and started doing some spot removing!

The command of the New Testament is: "Beloved . . . be diligent that ye may be found of him in peace, without spot, and blameless" (2 Pet. 3:14).

How To Go On

Keep on keeping clean.

Keep on testifying. Water must keep flowing.

Keep feeding on the Word.

Keep reading some devotional book—experiences of others who have lived gloriously.

Keep in the habit of praying regularly, so as to be in the spirit of prayer all the time.

Keep resisting the devil.

Keep cooperating with the Lord and obeying him (Acts 2:39).

Keep people whom you know need to be filled not only on your prayer list, but keep making opportunities to make them hungry and lead along those who are not.

Some Bewares

Do not ever get eyes on experiences.

Do not ever get eyes off the Giver and on the blessing. Charles Wesley: "I looked to Jesus and the dove of peace flew into my heart. I looked at the dove of peace and it flew away."

Do not ever backslide to the extent of seeking gifts.

Do not make your plans where you are to be shown off for the Lord.